# Cambridge Elements

Elements in Modern Wars

# ASYMMETRIC WARFARE

## Politics and Cultures of Violence in the Modern Era

Jacob Hagstrom
*Independent Researcher*

CAMBRIDGE
UNIVERSITY PRESS

Shaftesbury Road, Cambridge CB2 8EA, United Kingdom

One Liberty Plaza, 20th Floor, New York, NY 10006, USA

477 Williamstown Road, Port Melbourne, VIC 3207, Australia

314–321, 3rd Floor, Plot 3, Splendor Forum, Jasola District Centre,
New Delhi – 110025, India

103 Penang Road, #05–06/07, Visioncrest Commercial, Singapore 238467

Cambridge University Press is part of Cambridge University Press & Assessment,
a department of the University of Cambridge.

We share the University's mission to contribute to society through the pursuit of
education, learning and research at the highest international levels of excellence.

www.cambridge.org
Information on this title: www.cambridge.org/9781009567602

DOI: 10.1017/9781009567633



First published 2025

A catalogue record for this publication is available from the British Library

ISBN 978-1-009-56760-2 Hardback
ISBN 978-1-009-56764-0 Paperback
ISSN 2633-8378 (online)
ISSN 2633-836X (print)

# Asymmetric Warfare

## Politics and Cultures of Violence in the Modern Era

Elements in Modern Wars

DOI: 10.1017/9781009567633
First published online: May 2025

Jacob Hagstrom
*Independent Researcher*

**Author for correspondence:** Jacob Hagstrom, jacob.hagstrom@gmail.com

**Abstract:** The forces that fight asymmetric wars are so distinct that one side avoids direct military confrontation in favor of political, social, or otherwise unorthodox means of resistance. These conflicts have been a mainstay of modern times, though scholars have often separated them into various designations by era. Observers have referred, in chronological order, to Indian warfare, *petite guerre* (small war), *guerrilla* warfare, irregular or revolutionary war, and terrorism. The proliferation of labels over time has obscured the continuity of asymmetric wars throughout modernity. Stark distinctions in resources and capabilities have shaped the reasons why states and societies have decided to fight, and the manner in which they have fought. Across the modern era, mismatches arose in the domains of technology, intelligence production, and law. But in recent decades, so-called weak powers have neutralized many of the typical advantages of strong military states.

**Keywords:** military, guerrilla, war, revolution, terrorism



ISBNs: 9781009567602 (HB), 9781009567640 (PB), 9781009567633 (OC)
ISSNs: 2633-8378 (online), 2633-836X (print)

# Contents

# 1 Introduction: Learning from Unfair Fights

In the aftermath of the Napoleonic wars, French philosopher Victor Cousin concluded that leading military powers need not learn from primitive peoples. "A people is progressive only on the condition of war," Cousin announced. Those who had "sunk beneath the present time" could expect to be "blotted out from the book of life." According to this theory, the future was certain to belong to those most advanced in technology and efficient in bureaucracy. In short, there could be no need to study conflicts against so-called "barbarians."[1]

Across the Atlantic, American engineering professor Dennis Hart Mahan disagreed. In a lecture on "Indian Warfare" at West Point, he noted the "struggle of Spain against the genius of Napoleon" as one of many historical examples of "superior" militaries forced to adapt to less powerful opponents. The professor composed his work in response to the Seminoles' recent destruction of a column of U.S. regular soldiers in Florida, as seen in Figure 1. The solution to fighting asymmetric enemies was not "in imitating the institutions of other nations," but by adapting one's own "national character" to best suit the current threat. Mahan believed the U.S. army should not attempt to mimic Native American ways of war, but to apply "science and forethought," to learn from them and then outpace them.[2] For most of the two centuries since these men wrote, military thinkers have made an implicit agreement with Cousin; they ignored wars of the weak in favor of wars between great powers. But in the last generation, scholars have returned to the study of asymmetric conflicts: rebellions, insurgencies, and civil wars stretching back to the ancient period.

Ancient imperial forces understood the concept of asymmetry in warfare. Indeed, one of the earliest texts on war, the 5th-century-BC *Histories* of Herodotus, established a clear boundary between "Greeks" and "barbarians." For millennia, wars have produced unequal opponents and dehumanization of enemies. But asymmetric warfare took on its defining characteristics only in the modern era, with the confrontations between European invaders and the resistance they provoked in Africa, Asia, and the Americas. In this new imperial context, conflicts grew more asymmetric as they presented profound gaps between combatants in terms of technology, intelligence production, and law. Though ancient societies may have differed in these categories, the advantages that accrued to modern states brought about new, fundamental disparities. Scholars have tended to split these conflicts based on pejorative characteristics

---

[1] Victor Cousin, *The History of Philosophy*, Translated by Henning Linberg (Hilliard, 1832), 276, 281.

[2] Dennis Hart Mahan, "Indian Warfare," in *Composition of Armies* (USMA Special Collections, West Point, 1836), 33–36.

**Figure 1** Engraving, "Viewing the Demise of Major Dade and his Command in Florida," c. 1870, Wikimedia Commons

of the weaker side: *guerrillas* ("small" warriors unable to field heavy weapons), insurgents (rebels from within a recognized polity), irregulars (whose practices fall outside normative military practices), or terrorists (defined by inhumane tactics).

The concept of asymmetric warfare is preferable for two reasons. First, lumping conflicts together under the umbrella term of asymmetry reveals the continuity and centrality of wars between mismatched opponents to an American military tradition that predates the United States. Second, the details of these conflicts, laid out in chronological order, show that strong military forces have struggled more in recent decades, as so-called weak powers have found ways to neutralize defining modern asymmetries of technology, intelligence, and law.

Throughout the modern era, mismatches between strong and weak forces have not been deterministic for military outcomes; asymmetries have cut both ways. The "strong" military, though it enjoys the advantage of funds, and thus technology and firepower, often suffers from deficiencies of morale, and thus intelligence and manpower gathering capabilities. State militaries devote only a fraction of their resources to any given limited conflict, which for the weaker side becomes a total war, as the existential nature of defeat provokes ever more willingness to suffer casualties and escalate the means of violence employed. An initial asymmetry of resources cascades into asymmetries of political aims and political will.[3] The task of the counterinsurgents becomes more daunting, if expected, to quell all forms of rebellion in occupied territory, whereas the insurgency gains power the longer it survives. Or, as a frustrated Henry Kissinger quipped during the American War in Vietnam, "The conventional army loses if it does not win; the guerrilla wins if he does not lose."[4] The nature of these political imbalances has tended to limit the staying power of state military forces deployed abroad, especially if the government in question is a multiparty democracy vulnerable to opposition based on war weariness.

The study of warfare has gained special interest during periods in which it was practiced. Thus, analysis of asymmetric warfare proliferated in the post–Second World War era. Though the global conflict itself comprised mostly conventional combat, the end of the war unleashed the notable asymmetric means of nuclear weapons and national liberation movements. The successful Allied powers, fazed by popular politico-military movements in China, Southeast Asia, and North Africa, demanded some new theory of war to explain current events. Still, most academic attention concentrated on the novelty of nuclear warfare, and perhaps the nuclear focus was merited. Political scientists have posited that democracies tend not to go to war against other democracies. In economic terms, the Golden Arches theory sought to explain how the ties of global capitalism might prevent countries with McDonald's franchises from fighting one another.[5] But a better historical rule is that no two countries with nuclear arms have fought direct conflicts, if one sets aside minor border skirmishes on the Sino-Soviet and Indo-Pakistani frontiers.

Another crop of academic work on asymmetric warfare arrived in the 1990s, as American military thinkers sought to find a raison d'être after the collapse of the Soviet Union and the end of bipolar geopolitics. Newfound interest in wars of the weak surged alongside the U.S.-led Global War on Terrorism, which witnessed rapid conventional campaigns in Afghanistan and Iraq, both followed by long counterinsurgencies. The end of that latest conflict presents a good opportunity for a compilation of the existing scholarship, to continue the work of Dennis Hart Mahan in defiance of Victor Cousin types.

Though historians have understudied asymmetric wars compared to conventional operations, a series of historical agents have, like Professor Mahan, sought out previous accounts of mismatched opponents to understand their own times. These connections allow for a cyclical narrative, continuous across

---

[3] Andrew Mack, "Why Big Nations Lose Small Wars," *World Politics*, vol. 27, no. 2 (1975), 175–200, esp. 181–185.

[4] Henry Kissinger, "The Viet Nam Negotiations," *Foreign Affairs*, vol. 11, no. 2 (1969), 38–50.

[5] Thomas Friedman, *The Lexus and the Olive Tree: Understanding Globalization* (Farrar, Giroux, and Strauss, 1999).

the modern era, that consists of speculation about the future of warfare, experience of asymmetric conflicts, and reflection on how best to reform the military based on recent experience. Because of the dual status of the United States in the modern era – founded from an asymmetric conflict in the 18th century and patron of asymmetric wars since the 20th century – this study maintains an American emphasis, though situated in global context.

## 1.1 Definitions

All definitions have limits and exceptions. In the case of asymmetric warfare, the use of irregular methods in conventional interstate combat threatens to erode the distinctiveness of the concept. One may argue that "asymmetric war" is a redundant term, since all armed conflict contains an implicit quest for advantages over one's opponent. In this vein, the ancient Chinese philosopher Sun Tzu elaborated on his famous "know your enemy" maxim with a comment on creating uneven conditions. Knowledge about opponents was valuable because it enabled generals to attack their enemies' weak points with their own strengths.[6] Likewise, but in a modern context, Prussian theorist Carl von Clausewitz emphasized combatants' universal striving to produce inequality on the battlefield. Clausewitz derided military writers who described "unilateral action" by individual commanders, since warfare was really a "continuous interaction of opposites," not only in the fundamental sense of offense against defense, but of physical versus moral force, and scientific law versus genius that "rises above all rules."[7] Genius, in this philosophy, consisted in locating the decisive point of a battle and creating a local asymmetry of force at that point. Clausewitz wrote at a watershed moment in the history of asymmetric warfare, after the 18th-century development of "partisans," light, autonomous units that aided larger state-backed formations, and at the onset of the 19th-century "people's wars" that plagued the Napoleonic occupations.[8] The uses of unconventional methods, within interstate warfare and on its margins, demonstrated the tendency of conflicts to develop an asymmetric character over time, as political and military leadership looked for ways to gain advantage and end the period of physical combat on favorable, indeed unanswerable, terms.

Astute readers may object here that the definition of asymmetry may be loosened and stretched to fit almost any conflict. After all, no two military forces can be perfectly alike. If one side has more weapons or more effective

---

[6] Sun Tzu, *The Art of War*, Translated by Peter Harris (Knopf, 2018), 137.

[7] Carl von Clausewitz, *On War*, ed. Michael Howard and Peter Paret (Princeton University Press, 1976), 136–137.

[8] Sibylle Schiepers, *On Small War: Carl von Clausewitz and People's War* (Oxford University Press, 2018), 2–3.

technology than the other, does that side not possess an asymmetric advantage? It may be true that differences in weapons or other forms of technology have persisted across all armed conflicts. But the distinctiveness of asymmetric warfare emerges when one side has access not only to a better type of firearms, but to a more general capability, such as intercontinental logistics, long-distance communications, artillery, naval, or air forces, which their enemies lack. These are not differences of degree but of kind. At the outset of asymmetric wars, an imbalance of military force drives further divergences of ideals, expressed in the acquisition of intelligence, the motivation of recruits and supporters, or the redefinition of events according to particular moral or legal norms. These imbalances of morale and intelligence help to explain how movements that are weak in their initial manifestations gain strength over the course of conflicts. An international tipping point often occurs in these wars, as successful insurgent or secessionist movements tend to gain the intervention of friendly external sponsors, who typically seek not to impose their own systems but to sow chaos in the hinterlands of their opponents. Thus, asymmetric wars are not those in which two or more governments use violence to impose their own rival forms of order. Rather, they are conflicts in which one side seeks to impose order while the other fights for a freedom of ideals incompatible with the policies of state forces. Over the centuries, these sentiments of liberty have been expressed in terms as diverse as individual rights, communal privileges, or religious purity.

It may be useful at this point to illustrate how the concept of asymmetry here defined will apply to specific examples of combat across modern history, which comprise the content of the following sections. In the next part, Section 2, the Seven Years' War (1756–1763) becomes relevant for its contrast between British regular soldiers and Native American allies of the French, rather than the conventional battles fought by imperial troops in Europe and at Quebec. Likewise, the age of revolutions that followed is a subject for this volume not because of iconic American battles at Saratoga or Trenton, but due to the controversial role of militias in the war. The French experience during the era will concentrate on popular violence in the Vendée region (1793–1794) and during the Haitian revolution (1791–1804) rather than the Napoleonic battles among professional European armies at places like Austerlitz and Waterloo. Section 3 describes the long historical processes of colonization across the 19th and early 20th centuries, punctuated by wars fought by imperial armies of Britain, France, the United States, Russia, and the Netherlands against local indigenous polities. In Section 4, the world wars of the 20th century, like those of the 18th century, receive selective treatment as they apply to asymmetric warfare. The analysis touches on the First World War for its tribal and colonial rebellions in Africa and the Middle East rather than the industrial combat of the

Western and Eastern European fronts. Asymmetric conflicts abounded during the interwar period, as well, and this volume highlights the roles of the Irish War for Independence (1920–1921) and the Second Italo-Ethiopian War (1935–1937) to reveal the limits of European imperial power. The Second World War enters as a topic of study not for its armored clashes between Germany and the Soviet Union, nor its naval battles between the United States and Japan, but for the new, fundamental asymmetry that the war created in terms of nuclear weapons, as well as the multitude of armed resistance groups that continued to fight hostile state forces into the "postwar" period in places such as China, Greece, and the Philippines. Asymmetric warfare proliferated in the neo-imperial age of Cold War superpower competition, described in Section 5. Special interest applies to combat in Korea, Vietnam, and Afghanistan that was waged between forces growing apart in their resources: elite, often clandestine, government units on one hand and people's militias on the other. This trend toward mismatched combatants continued despite the end of the Cold War, due to the U.S.-led efforts in the Global War on Terrorism, which is the focus of Section 6. Though asymmetric wars often emerged on the peripheries of strong states and their spheres of influence, it should be clear from their frequent occurrence and lasting consequences that these conflicts were central to the modern state system.

Official attempts to define asymmetric warfare revived early in the 21st century, after what seemed to be decisive military operations by U.S.-led coalitions in Afghanistan and Iraq failed to bring about projected political results. The resulting attempts to create new doctrine offered a window into the military mindset. One U.S. army officer with recent combat experience defined asymmetric conflict in a 2006 policy paper as

> population-centric, nontraditional warfare waged between a militarily superior power and one or more inferior powers, which encompasses all the following aspects: evaluating and defeating the asymmetric threat, conducting asymmetric operations, understanding cultural asymmetry and evaluating asymmetric cost.[9]

This expansive practitioner's definition continued to emphasize conventional military dimensions of conflict, as it placed the enemy threat first, a problem to be solved by operations. The specificity of this kind of warfare only becomes evident with the definition's meta-operational categories of culture and cost. The official U.S. counterinsurgency doctrine issued in 2007 substituted "irregular" for "asymmetric" as a descriptor, but the concept is apparent in the manual's

---

[9] David Buffaloe, "Defining Asymmetric Warfare," *The Land Warfare Papers*, no. 58 (September 2006), 17.

section on the "nature of insurgency," which reads: "Insurgent groups tend to adopt an irregular approach because they initially lack the resources required to directly confront the incumbent government in traditional warfare."[10] Never mind that insurgency is as traditional a type of warfare as Americans can claim. The central concept remains fixed on imbalances, not only in resources and capabilities, but also in the intangibles of the conflict's meaning amongst the population.

An asymmetric war may be defined in the most basic way as a conflict in which the differences between opponents cause them to operate in unique ways. French theorist David Galula used the analogy of a fight between a lion and a fly to illustrate the point; the fly cannot stomp on the lion, and the lion cannot fly. The fly has no hope of beating the lion outright, but it may buzz around the lion's mane and drive it mad with exhaustion.[11] In these conflicts, combatants do not agree about the meaning of the conflict, are not armed with the same kinds of weapons, and do not behave alike.

The difficulty to categorize combat into neat boxes since the end of the Second World War has led some authors to reject the oft-cited trinity by which Clausewitz described the roles of the state, the military, and the people. Modern warfare, these critics allege, blends these categories to the point they are no longer useful. War has changed its fundamental nature because at a certain point, it began to result from the actions of irrational, non-state agents, rather than employed as an instrument of state policy.[12] Recent authors have instead proposed a "hybrid warfare" model, in which (legal) interstate conflict occurs alongside (illegal) insurgency waged by civilians. The scope of this work allows us to see that many wars throughout the modern era produced both symmetrical and asymmetrical theaters, as the First World War gave rise to trenches as well as tribal insurgencies. The recent emphasis on "lawfare," or perceived unfairness of enemies who refuse to play by existing rules, betrays what one critic called "a convenient self-delusion" of the West: that wars can be limited by agreed-upon constraints.[13] The American defense community's reaction to Chinese military officers' publication of *Unrestricted Warfare*

---

[10] *Counterinsurgency* (JP 3–24) xi (April 25, 2018).

[11] David Galula, *Counterinsurgency Warfare: Theory and Practice* (1964), xii (Westport, CT: Praeger Security International, 1964).

[12] Others Have Argued for the Continued Relevance of Clausewitz for Modern, Irregular Wars; See Scheipers, *On Small War;* Hew Strachan and Andreas Herberg-Rothe, *Clausewitz in the Twenty-First Century* (Oxford University Press, 2007), 1–10; Antulio Echevarria II, *Clausewitz and Contemporary War* (Oxford University Press, 2007).

[13] Frank Hoffman, "Hybrid Warfare and Challenges," *Joint Forces Quarterly* 52 (2009), 34–48; for "lawfare," see Charles Dunlap, "Lawfare Today: A Perspective," *Yale Journal of International Affairs*, 146 (Winter 2008), 146–154; Roger Barnett, *Asymmetrical Warfare: Today's Challenge to U.S. Military Power* (Potomac Books, 2003), 15; for the apt critique, see Robert Johnson,

(1999), which called for economic, infrastructure, and social attacks in future conflicts, could only be so intense and negative if one ignored the various Cold War forms of soft power that Americans pursued with relish.[14] Indeed, asymmetric warfare, and the spilling over of military violence into economic and cultural conflict, have been a chronic condition for North Americans since the arrival of Europeans to the continent.

## 2 Asymmetry and Revolutions (1492–1815)

Revolutions bookended the early modern period, as first military and then political affairs underwent sweeping changes. The military revolutions that took place between the 14th and 16th centuries replaced small feudal armies with larger formations of professional troops, equipped with firearms and artillery pieces. European monarchs, to pay for their new militaries, increased burdens on their subjects, who eventually rebelled against their oppressors. The American, French, and Haitian political revolutions, results of 18th-century financial crises, proved successful against stronger imperial military forces. The wars opened opportunities for initially marginal groups to use narratives of human rights in their struggles against the dominant monarchical political order.

## 2.1 Revolutions in Military Affairs (RMA)

Historians have debated the nature and the scope of European military competition in the early modern period. What were the key innovations through which strong military states emerged in Sweden, Spain, France, Austria, and England? Participants in the RMA debate argue that the enormous expenses of defensive fortifications and wall-destroying artillery motivated the development of the fiscal-military state. In this new system, monarchs no longer raised war funds ad hoc from a collection of liege lords, but instead organized a bureaucratized tax apparatus. Armies dominated by noble cavalrymen paid in fief gave way to bourgeois armies of infantry, artillery, and engineers paid in cash or credit. Other historians noted that the fiscal-military state had its most significant applications in the building of transoceanic navies that European states – Portugal,

---

"Hybrid War and Its Countermeasures: A Critique of the Literature," *Small Wars and Insurgencies*, vol. 29, no. 1 (2017), 141–163.

[14] Qiao Liang and Wang Xiangsui, *Unrestricted Warfare* (People's Liberation Army Press, 1999); see also Shen Kuiguan, "Dialectics of Defeating the Superior with the Inferior," in Michael Pillsbury, ed., *Chinese Views of Future Warfare* (National Defense University Press, 1997), 213–220; David Barno and Nora Benashel, "A New Generation of Unrestricted Warfare," *War on the Rocks*, 19 April 2016.

Spain, France, and especially England – developed in competition with each other during the 16th and 17th centuries.[15]

Whatever the specifics of the timing and causation of military revolutions, the voluminous debate addresses a basic question. How was it that a small contingent of Europeans deployed armies to America, Africa, and Asia, and not the other way around? The logic of empire depended on an asymmetric military situation, as imperial agents leveraged three unique capabilities: to come and go by sea, to bombard targets with naval forces, and to import firearms for combat on land.

Another significant aspect of asymmetry was disease, as Europeans brought "virgin soil epidemics" to the Americas. Military expeditions from Europe throughout the 16th and 17th centuries encountered indigenous societies reeling from demographic crises, though resistance movements soon adapted to the conditions of the creole societies that emerged. The European new-comers, by coincidence, had bypassed much of their own catastrophic plagues by the late 15th century. Thereafter, some European societies began to produce merchant classes and population surpluses that sought opportunities abroad. As these processes of demographic and economic expansion took place, military reformers adapted scientific discoveries into specific technologies in metallurgy for guns, chemistry for powder, and astronomy for trans-oceanic navigation.[16]

Spanish and Portuguese military expeditions of the 15th and 16th centuries sought to overawe indigenous Americans into submission without the need for pitched battle. The *conquistadors* were so outnumbered by indigenous people that they could not so much conquer, as their label implied, as intervene into existing wars among American societies. The combination of the Iberians' technology and their local allies' intelligence wrought brutal results for those indigenous communities that resisted demands for their resources and their souls.[17] The Iberian destruction of American communities provoked a political propaganda campaign in England known as the Black Legend. The Franciscan priest Las Casas recorded the cruelty of the early American conquests, which served as justification for

---

[15] Geoffrey Parker, *The Military Revolution: Military Innovation and the Rise of the West, 1500-1800* (Cambridge University Press, 1988); Clifford Rogers, ed. *The Military Revolution Debate: Readings on the Military Transformation of Early Modern Europe* (Westview Press, 1995); N. A.M. Rodger, "From the 'Military Revolution' to the 'Fiscal-Naval State,'" *Journal of Maritime Research*, vol. 13, no. 2 (Nov. 2011), 119–128.

[16] Alfred Crosby, "Virgin Soil Epidemics as a Factor in the Aboriginal Depopulation in America," *William and Mary Quarterly*, vol. 30 (1976), 289–299; David Jones, "Virgin Soils Revisited," *William and Mary Quarterly*, vol. 60 (October 2003), 703–742; Paul Kelton, *Epidemics and Enslavement: Biological Catastrophe in the Native Southeast* (University of Nebraska Press, 2007).

[17] Felipe Fernandez-Armesto, *Columbus* (Oxford University Press, 1991); Matthew Restall, *Seven Myths of the Spanish Conquest* (Oxford University Press, 2003).

Britons to impinge on Spanish claims and, in theory, to create more benevolent colonial conditions.[18] From indigenous perspectives, there was often precious little difference in outcome among the various European colonial policies.

## 2.2 Ways of War

It is difficult to assess how the introduction of European technologies to America affected indigenous ways of war, though anthropologists and historians have offered several theories. The oldest scholarship on the subject argued that Native American warfare had been ceremonial in nature, and that the introduction of firearms transformed and intensified warfare.[19] More recent studies have made two significant revisions: first, that innovation was a two-way street; and second, that pre-contact American warfare had a robust tradition of lethality. The 17th-century English adapted indigenous tools and practices such as snowshoes, aimed fire, and "skulking" behind cover and concealment, rather than fighting in line formations on open fields.[20] Moreover, indigenous warfare did produce significant casualties in certain conditions. Native Americans of the eastern woodlands employed a "cutting off" way of war, rather than pitched battles, that minimized the likelihood of human losses while it maximized the social goals of warfare: taking captives, avenging past casualties, or raiding for material gain.

Though the means of cutting off enemies was scalable, from ambushes of a few travelers to attacks on large settlements, violence in indigenous American societies tended to be limited by several factors. Concepts of revenge were circumscribed: one or two enemies killed or captured could cover the losses of a previous campaign season. Europeans, on the other hand, often avenged the killings of individuals with escalation to the destruction of entire villages, as colonial English troops did at Mystic, Connecticut, in 1637 during the Pequot War. Furthermore, indigenous political leadership was more persuasive than coercive. War chiefs lacked their European counterparts' capacity to summon troops by combinations of force and finance, so Native American coalitions relied on charisma and offers to win prestige; their war parties thus tended to be small and local in composition. Furthermore, war chiefs of the eastern woodlands shared power with

---

[18] Bernard Bailyn, *Atlantic History: Concepts and Contours* (Harvard University Press, 2005); John H. Elliot, *Empires of the Atlantic: Britain and Spain in America 1492-1830* (Yale University Press, 2006).

[19] Harry Holbert Turney-High, *Primitive War: Its Practice and Concepts* (University of South Carolina Press, 1949); Quincy Wright, *A Study of War* (University of Chicago Press, 1942).

[20] Patrick Malone, *The Skulking Way of War: Technology and Tactics among the New England Indians* (Madison Books, 1991).

"Peace Chiefs," who dispatched resident aliens to neighboring communities as diplomats to prevent minor conflicts from escalating. In short, European firearms did not introduce lethality to Native American warfare, but they offered a new possibility for lethality during battles, after operational surprise had been lost.[21]

## 2.3 The Seven Years' War (1756–1763)

Throughout the 18th century, the French boasted an advantage over the British in terms of indigenous allies, who supplied the bulk of manpower and intelligence in North America. French success in recruiting indigenous peoples resulted from settler economics. By the 1750s, there were only fifty thousand French people on the continent, compared to one and a half million with ties to Britain. Indigenous societies identified the less intrusive of the rival empires and tended to support the French or remain neutral during conflicts between the Europeans. Native Americans used distinctive tactics in battle: the element of surprise through concealment, ambush, and aimed fire, a hit-and-run style of fighting "in the woods." The British overcame their deficiencies in this mode of fighting as they learned to lean on their powerful navy to launch bombardments and amphibious landings, for which the French and their indigenous allies had little response.[22]

In 1755, British General Edward Braddock arrived in America and attempted to build a road through the Appalachian forest to threaten French forts of the region. He soon found himself waylaid by indigenous fighters. Some historians have argued the British sent the wrong types of troops for this country, as regular heavy infantry plodded into ambushes set by nimbler foes. Colonel George Washington, a staff officer at the battle of Monongahela, disagreed and blamed the loss on a lack of nerve within Braddock's formations. Washington's lesson was not that the British should have been more prepared for irregular light troops, but that they should have been more regular and disciplined in their training.[23] Braddock's 44th and 48th regiments of foot had been dispersed for constabulary duty in Ireland before their voyage to America. Both units were understrength by about half and had to recruit raw soldiers just before embarkation. The French and their indigenous allies, after days of careful scouting, performed a series of decentralized encirclements of the British line. The

---

[21] Wayne Lee, *The Cutting-Off Way: Indigenous Warfare in Eastern North America, 1500-1800* (University of North Carolina Press, 2023).

[22] Fred Anderson, *Crucible of War: The Seven Years' War and the Fate of Empire in British North America 1754-1766* (Knopf, 2001), 12–14.

[23] John Hall, "An Irregular Reconsideration of George Washington and the American Military Tradition," *Journal of Military History*, vol. 78 (July 2014), 961–993, here 962.

documentary record of British survivors indicates the psychological effects of the indigenous fighters' rapid movement, as well as the terrifying sounds of war cries and expectations of mutilation upon captivity. The tactical reversal turned into a rout.[24]

Following their defeat at the outset of combat on North America, the British military redeemed itself over the ensuing course of the Seven Years' War. Three years after the disaster on the Monongahela, a new column under Colonel Henri Bouquet succeeded where Braddock had failed, as troops built a road from the western British settlements to Fort Duquesne. The British successes took place in the absence of France's indigenous allies, most of whom had left the war by the end of 1758. Bouquet, whose previous experience had been limited to Europe, drew lessons from what he called a "new kind of war."[25] In a pamphlet entitled "Reflections on the War with the Savages of North America," he noted that Europeans were used to fighting in a "cultivated and inhabited" land, which featured roads, armaments magazines, and hospitals, as well as "a generous enemy to yield to" in normal conditions. On the other hand, Bouquet emphasized:

> In an American campaign, everything is terrible; the face of the country, the climate, the enemy. There is no refreshment for the healthy, nor relief for the sick. A vast, unhospitable desart, unsafe and treacherous, surrounds them, where victories are not decisive, but defeats are ruinous; and simple death is the least misfortune which can happen to them.

A lack of intelligence made the hostile environment still more forbidding. Since the indigenous fighters seemed to compound their advantages in intelligence with an ability to fight "scattered" rather than in a "compact body," Bouquet suggested three maxims for a European army engaged in America. He counseled they be "lightly cloathed, armed and accoutered," that they avoid "close order" formations, and that they learn to operate "with great rapidity," to address the Native Americans' skill at moving through the forest.[26]

The frustrations brought on by indigenous soldiers' mobility led Bouquet to seek extraordinary methods. In a 1764 letter to William Penn, Bouquet asked not only for a unit of "light horse," which had served well during the Forbes expedition of 1758, but also one hundred "proper Hounds," to be imported from Britain with their handlers. Bouquet speculated that the dogs would be useful to

---

[24] David Preston, *The Other Face of Battle: America's Forgotten Wars and the Experience of Combat*, ed. Wayne Lee (Oxford University Press, 2021), 31–64.

[25] William Smith, *Historical Account of Bouquet's Expedition against the Ohio Indians in 1764* (Robert Clarke, 1907), 83.

[26] Smith, *Bouquet's Expedition*, 13, 16, 90–1; for Bouquet's historical allusions to Caesar in Africa and the "hussar" cavalry of Eastern Europe, see 87–8.

"discover the Ambushes of the Enemy, and direct the Pursuit."[27] There was no indication in subsequent correspondence that the animals supplied the benefits Bouquet imagined, but his logic revealed an attempt to overcome the mobility gap with technical solutions imported from the metropole.

The most heinous example of this trend, popularized to the point of cliché, was British General Jeffery Amherst's order to gift blankets discarded by a smallpox hospital to Shawnee adversaries who besieged Fort Pitt in 1763. On that occasion, Amherst counseled his subordinate Bouquet to use not only biological warfare, but animals used for hunting, and "Every Strategem in our power to Reduce them."[28] The military effectiveness of the blankets, as with the dogs, was unclear. The more significant factor that ended Pontiac's rebellion was the British diplomatic promise to keep settlers east of a Proclamation line that ran along the peaks of the Appalachian Mountains. Bouquet demonstrated the power of letters to government officials. His epistolary efforts to bring about the Proclamation revealed the early importance of communications media for the building of coalitions and consensus to end asymmetric warfare.[29]

## 2.4 The Age of Revolutions

Rebellions in British North America, France, and Haiti resulted in extended periods of warfare. According to some historians, these conflicts introduced a new type of conflict fought by a new class of soldier: "total war" waged by fighters who rallied to popular, idealistic causes. The levée en masse in France forms the paradigm for this concept of novelty in warfare during the Age of Revolutions.[30] But claims that the political upheavals of the late 18th century brought about total war have obscured a continuity from the colonial era: asymmetric conflicts had been total to the colonized side throughout the previous centuries.

The Age of Revolutions represented a rupture in political, rather than military, history, as the trends of early modern "military revolutions" continued with the development of fiscal-military states. American rebel leader George Washington, for example, sought to emulate the army of the British Empire rather than to

---

[27] *The Papers of Henry Bouquet*, ed. Louis M. Waddell, vol. VI, November 1761–July 1765 (Historical and Museum Commission, 1994), 554–555, 563.

[28] John Grenier, *The First Way of War: American War Making on the Frontier, 1607-1814* (Cambridge University Press, 2005), 144; Elizabeth Fenn, "Biological Warfare in Eighteenth Century North America: Beyond Jeffery Amherst," *Journal of American History*, vol. 86 (2000), 1552–1580.

[29] Konstantin Dierks, *In My Power: Letter Writing and Communications in Early America* (University of Pennsylvania Press, 2009), 125–127.

[30] David Bell, *The First Total War: Napoleon's Europe and the Birth of Warfare as We Know It* (Houghton Mifflin, 2007), 9; Russell Weigley, *The Age of Battles: The Quest for Decisive Warfare from Breitenfeld to Waterloo* (Indiana University Press, 1991), 290.

innovate beyond it. Revolutionary and Napoleonic-era soldiers, as their letters demonstrate, were no more idealistic than those who served the French monarchy had been, but the new state recruited them faster and from a larger social pool. The biggest difference between Napoleon's armies and those of his ancien régime predecessors was size, rather than methods or equipment.[31] New empires across the Atlantic oppressed those outside the body politic on par with royalist rivals, though lines of exclusion defined status more by race and gender than class, as in the old monarchies. The end of the 18th century witnessed a proliferation, rather than the introduction, of "citizen-soldier" militias, rapidly formed, light infantry skirmishers that had been long been commonplace on battlefields in Europe and America.[32]

### 2.4.1 The American Revolution

The U.S. War for Independence began with battles at two small Massachusetts towns in April 1775, over a year before the rebels declared political independence from the British Empire. Social protest, however, had been brewing in North America since the end of the Seven Years' War. The financial burdens of the late conflict against the French fell unfairly, some began to claim, on those without representation in Parliament. Though popular narratives tended to emphasize the actions of rebel leader Samuel Adams and his associates in the Sons of Liberty, an intelligence network designed to stymie oppressive British governance, political violence during the 1760s also took place between rival groups of colonists. Fighting broke out between coastal elites and a variety of rural leveling protest movements, such as the Regulators of North Carolina. Moreover, the idealism that men such as Samuel Adams and his cousin John lent to the colonial insurgency has overshadowed the material interests in question. Colonists tended to care less about political abstractions and more about discrete policies that governed western land and British credit. These issues, under the guise of "liberty," drove Virginia's gentry into rebellion by 1776, to the benefit of the Patriot movement in New England.[33]

American rebels fought the first three years of the conflict at decided material disadvantages. Washington preferred to correct the balance by making the American rebels look and act more like their British foes, to train them according to the dictates of Prussian officer Baron von Steuben, in the hopes of waging

---

[31] Alan Forrest, *Napoleon's Men: The Soldiers of the Revolution and Empire* (Hambledon and London, 2002), 3–9.

[32] Roger Chickering and Stig Forster, eds., *War in an Age of Revolution: 1775-1815* (Cambridge University Press, 2010), 12.

[33] Woody Holton, *Forced Founders: Indians, Debtors, Slaves and the Making of the American Revolution in Virginia* (University of North Carolina Press, 1999).

offensive operations against other regulars.[34] Yet Washington also recognized the reality that he had to wage a defensive conflict fought for the most part by "irregular" or short-time troops. Therefore, he called on Congress at the end of 1776 to create a "respectable" army that would be "competent to every exigency," both *grande guerre* against British regulars and *petite guerre* against Native Americans and Loyalist militias. One of Washington's top subordinates, General Charles Lee, disagreed and thought the American rebels should lean into potential asymmetric advantages. Lee raised the possibility of dispersing squads of regulars among the towns and farms, to lead partisans and drag the British into a bloodier civil war. Except in small pockets of the American South later in the war, Lee's vision found little support among the rebel leadership.[35]

In strategic terms, the colonists' asymmetric war against the British Empire became symmetrical after the French alliance of 1778. With this diplomatic achievement, Americans gained the capability to counter the British navy and to pay soldiers on the brink of desertion. These elements came together during the decisive 1781 Yorktown campaign, fought by a combined Franco-American army and enabled by a French loan and naval blockade.[36] Rather than foreign aid, the popular mythology of the "minuteman" held that the common American citizen-soldier had stymied the regular British redcoats and forced the empire to abandon its reconquest of America. This populist-patriotic narrative omits Washington's frequent quips about the militia's lack of dependability, that to rely on them was to rest "on a broken staff," that they were "ready to fly from their own Shadows," and amounted to only the "garnish of the table" compared to the regulars of the Continental Army and their French allies.[37] While there were some instances of successful militia action, they tended to result from charismatic small unit leadership, as in the case of "Swamp Fox" Francis Marion.[38] As a whole, militia performance was variable, and their short enlistments meant they tended more toward waste and loss than regulars.

But militias did lend some benefits to Washington. First, they comprised the bulk of his forces – anywhere from three quarters to 90 percent of troops in the field at any given time. Militiamen, even when they were not active on campaign, served as a network of intelligence and communication that favored the Patriots,

---

[34] Charles Royster, *A Revolutionary People at War: The Continental Army and American Character* (University of North Carolina Press, 1979), 213–214.

[35] John Shy, *A People Numerous and Armed: Reflections on the Military Struggle for American Independence* (University of Michigan Press, 1990), 133–162.

[36] Howard Peckham, *The War for Independence: A Military History* (University of Chicago Press, 1979), 164–182.

[37] Washington to Hancock, 25 September 1776; John Pancake, *This Destructive War: The British Campaign in the Carolinas, 1780-1782* (University of Alabama Press, 1985), 132.

[38] Russell Weigley, *The Partisan War: The South Carolina Campaign of 1780-1782* (University of South Carolina Press, 1975).

and their presence dissuaded Loyalists from organizing a counterinsurgency. British soldiers became frustrated with parsing out militia leadership from bandits and criminals. When British regulars acted harshly against these figures, the popular backlash hurt the cause of reintegrating rebels back into the empire.[39]

Washington's army, rather than augment partisan warfare, became more professional over time. The course of Daniel Morgan's career was illustrative in this respect. His rifle companies that arrived at Boston from the Pennsylvania woods performed poorly in early skirmishes. But by the battle of Cowpens in 1781, Morgan understood how to coordinate the use of militias as sharpshooters and light infantry scouts on the margins of regular infantry formations. Morgan's units represented, per historian John Hall, "the maturation of the American ranger tradition," from "irregular antecedents" to "elite regulars."[40]

### 2.4.2 The French Revolution

Across the Atlantic, the American War for Independence shook French finances. The debt that King Louis XVI's government incurred to support the war effort proved too much to handle, as the French state was already burdened by the costs of the recent Seven Years' War. The failure of the fiscal-military state, rather than desperate class warfare waged by peasants, opened the door to the French Revolution, led in its early years by "enlightened" nobles. When the revolution became more radical with the execution of the royals in 1793, France fractured into civil war.

The most intense asymmetric conflict emerged in the Vendée, a coastal region south of the Loire valley. Resentments had long simmered among religious, rural inhabitants against the revolutionaries in Paris, and open rebellion broke out with a request for troops in March. It was one thing to become citizens of a secular republic and watch it attack God and King from afar, and still another to be asked to fight for it.[41] Rather than submit to a draft, thousands of young men organized a White Catholic force to oppose the revolutionary, Blue-clad troops.

After conventional attempts against rebels failed, radical followers of Jacques-Rene Hébert in the National Convention demanded an intensification

---

[39] Matthew Ward, "The American Militias: The Garnish of a Table?" in Roger Chickering and Stig Forster, eds., *War in an Age of Revolution, 1775–1815* (Cambridge: Cambridge University Press, 2010), 165–174.

[40] Hall, "Irregular Reconsideration," 980–986.

[41] David Bell, *The First Total War: Napoleon's Europe and the Birth of Warfare as We Know It* (Houghton Mifflin, 2007), 165–166; for early recognition of unpopularity of the levée en masse, see Hans Delbruck, *The Dawn of Modern Warfare*, History of the Art of War, vol. IV (University of Nebraska Press, 1990), 395.

of violence. General Louis-Marie Turreau traversed the territory with 3,000 men, who marched through the Vendée in a systematic way, according to Convention orders of August 1793, "to exterminate this rebel race, to destroy their hiding-places, to burn their forests, to cut down their crops." These orders became irrelevant after Republican victories broke up the rebel army in battles during October and December, yet Turreau persisted in his "military promenade" across the defenseless population in the early months of 1794. He claimed afterward to have been less afraid of local insurgents than of his political overlords, the *Hébertistes* known for sending generals who lacked ambition to the guillotine. By 1795, when the new French commander Lazare Hoche turned to a more conciliatory pacification effort, a quarter of the region's population had been killed.[42]

Of course, there had been many previous examples of violence against noncombatants in French history: the Camisard revolt in the early 18th century, religious wars of the 16th century, and the crusade against Cathar heretics before that. But the French monarchs and their military captains tended to use war as a limited, legal means of solving political problems. The Revolutionary government transformed warfare by seeking an escalation of participation from society. Opponents of the new regime, based on Enlightenment principles assumed to be universal, could only be "enemies of liberty," per National Convention deputy Maximilien Robespierre, "monsters of the universe." Warfare was no longer the recourse of nobles to resolve petty disputes; it had been reimagined as a fight to the death between peoples.[43] As the revolutionaries ceded their chaotic reign to the stability of dictatorship under Napoleon, the emperor inherited their concept of greater societal participation in war.

Napoleon's dazzling battlefield victories have overshadowed the extent to which peasant rebellions laid low his empire. The term "guerrilla" (small warrior) first emerged in Napoleonic Spain to describe the fanatical attacks of peasants and religious leaders who at times cooperated with the Spanish government-in-exile, and still less often with foreign allies in Britain and Portugal. It was the ideological commitment of the fighters (not merely opportunistic criminals or rioters) and their lack of direct connection to a sovereign patron that separated the Spanish insurgents from predecessors. Their role was to oppose legal power, rather than to act as an auxiliary of it, as partisan units had during the Seven Years' War.[44]

---

[42] Bell, *First Total War*, 156, 161, 179.

[43] John Q. Whitman, *Verdict of Battle: The Law of Victory and the Making of Modern War* (Harvard University Press, 2012); Maximilien Robespierre, "On the Enemies of the Nation," speech of 26 May 1794.

[44] Sandrine Picaud-Monnerat, *La Petite Guerre au XVIIIe Siècle* (Economica, 2010), esp. 40.

Napoleon's short-lived occupations of Spain, Italy, and various German territories demonstrated the significance of religion as a martial motivation, as faith engendered feelings of national difference in opposition to the Revolutionary concepts of universality and rational bureaucracy. Thus, national secessionist sentiment was less the cause of revolutions as a result of the chaos that war and occupation brought about. The nation became the idiom of insurgency for those opposed to more intrusive empires. The printing press became a weapon, as revolutionaries saw their role as educating the people about the as-yet-unrealized nation.[45]

### 2.4.3 The Haitian Revolution

Nowhere in the Atlantic was the rupture from colony to nation more sudden and painful than in French Saint-Domingue, reborn as the Empire of Haiti. A population of 400,000 enslaved people rebelled against some 50,000 white and mixed-race elites, and the pent-up resentments of slavery fueled atrocities. Some owners exacerbated the destruction by arming their laborers, out of fear their plantations would be overrun in the revolutionary struggle between republicans and royalists. A major turning point in the rebellion came in 1793, when republican agents promised freedom to former slaves in exchange for military service. Toussaint L'Ouverture and a group of fellow generals gained power by subverting the royalist hierarchy, and they pledged loyalty to the new revolutionary French government.[46]

But when Napoleon came to power, he was disturbed by the relative independence of the former plantation overseer L'Ouverture, depicted in Figure 2. The emperor deployed his brother-in-law, General Charles Leclerc, to overthrow the territory's leadership. As French reinforcements approached the island, L'Ouverture reminded a subordinate of their asymmetric means of defense, as he counseled, "We have no other resource than destruction and fire. Bear in mind that the soil bathed with our sweat must not furnish our enemies with the smallest sustenance."[47] The French repaid atrocity with atrocity. Leclerc ordered troops to "destroy all the blacks of the mountains – men and women – and spare only children under twelve years of age."[48] One of his subordinates, by contrast, advocated a departure from harsh French

---

[45] Jeremy Adelman, "An Age of Imperial Revolutions," *American Historical Review*, vol. 113, no. 2 (April 2008), 319–340, esp. 319–320.

[46] Laurent Dubois, *Avengers of the New World: The Story of the Haitian Revolution* (Harvard University Press, 2004), 134–135; Jeremy Popkin, *You Are All Free: The Haitian Revolution and the Abolition of Slavery* (Cambridge University Press, 2010), 10, 385–386.

[47] Dubois, *Avengers*, 179.

[48] Claude Auguste and Marcel Auguste, *L'Éxpedition Leclerc* (Henri Deschamps, 1985), 236; Sibylle Scheipers, *Unlawful Combatants: A Genealogy of the Irregular Fighter* (Oxford University Press, 2015), 154.

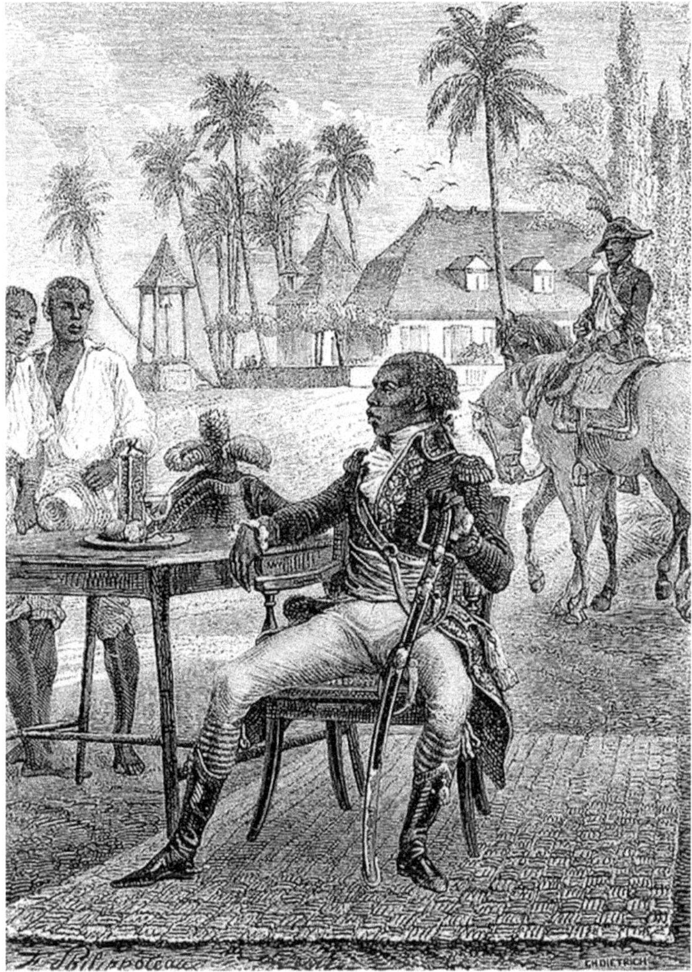

**Figure 2** Engraving of Toussaint L'Ouverture by Felix Philippoteaux, 1870, Wikimedia Commons

practices, which included crucifixion and feeding to dogs. Bertrand Clauzel, in a more productive course, bought up plantations "to engage [the inhabitants] in reconstruction," in a work-for-loyalty program that became standard practice much later, during 20th- and 21st-century counterinsurgencies.[49] Despite promising signs for the project, Clauzel did not remain long enough to see lasting results. Within a month of his departure, workers abandoned their fields and

---

[49] Bertrand Clauzel, *Explications du maréchal Clauzel* (Ambroise Dupont, 1837), 96–97; Philippe Girard, *The Slaves Who Beat Napoleon: Toussaint L'Ouverture and the Haitian War for Independence, 1801-1804* (University of Alabama Press, 2011), 212, 301.

rejoined the rebellion. The following year, they achieved their independence in the first successful revolt of enslaved people in the Atlantic world.

### 2.4.4 Revolutionary Coda: War of 1812

The pressures of war against Napoleonic France pushed the British to impress, or abduct, American sailors at sea. The British claimed that their captives were in fact royal subjects who had fled service in U.S. ports. Nevertheless, the slight to American sovereignty, along with British refusals to cede fortifications in the West, led the U.S. Congress to declare war. The Americans planned, as in the War for Independence, on an overland strategy to conquer Canada, but the conflict turned out to be a battle of survival for the experimental republican government. Even in the symmetrical theaters against "civilized" opponents, the war brought atrocities and unconventional tactics: the burning of capitals York and Washington, the execution of prisoners, and the British enticement of enslaved people throughout the Chesapeake Bay region to serve as an "internal enemy."[50] But while the U.S. army developed into more regular formations under General Winfield Scott in the north, General Andrew Jackson followed a different course in the southern theater, as he intervened in the Creek Civil War.

The famous U.S. victory at the Battle of New Orleans (1815) overshadowed the historical importance of Jackson's previous battle at Horseshoe Bend (Tohopeka, 1814), which he viewed as "avenging" the massacre of white settlers and their indigenous allies at Fort Mims. Jackson led a collection of regular infantry, Tennessee militia, and Native American allies on a typical "feed fight" expedition, in which troops burned crops and settlements until they hemmed in the "Red Stick" Creek resistance movement to a narrow river bend. Jackson's troops were ruthless in the ensuing battle, as they massacred some 800 Creek fighters, along with many women, at a loss of only 70 to their own side. Jackson spared neither his defeated foe nor his own Lower Creek allies. After the battle, the Creek confederation ceded land that became half the state of Alabama and much of Georgia to the United States. Some of the surviving "Red Stick" Creek families fled south to Florida, where they would participate in the Second Seminole War (1835–1842) during Jackson's presidency.[51]

---

[50] Alan Taylor, *The Civil War of 1812: American Citizens, British Subjects, Irish Rebels, and Indian Allies* (Knopf, 2011); Taylor, *The Internal Enemy: Slavery and War in Virginia, 1772–1832* (W.W. Norton, 2013).

[51] J. M. Opal, *Avenging the People: Andrew Jackson, the Rule of Law, and the American Nation* (Oxford University Press, 2017); Robert G. Thrower, "Causalities and Consequences of the Creek War: A Modern Creek Perspective," in Kathryn Braund, ed., *Tohopeka: Rethinking the Creek War and the War of 1812* (University of Alabama Press, 2012), 26.

The military campaigns that Jackson led during the War of 1812 and the subsequent First Seminole War (1818–1819) opened up the Old Southwest to settlement by white planters, which allowed the creation of the Cotton Kingdom and generated the rationale for his later Indian Removal legislation. Jackson had become the latest in a series of "men on horseback," leaders such as Washington, Napoleon, and L'Ouverture, whose military exploits propelled them to become heads of state. The imposing cults of personality they cultivated served to overawe colonized opponents and loyal citizens alike.[52] In the Age of Revolutions, participation in the asymmetric warfare of imperial forces became pathways to fame and power.

Throughout the 19th century, European politics underwent a gradual shift from chaotic revolutions to the management of relative stability. As a balance of power settled on the continent, the culture of empire shifted as well, from an Enlightenment ethos that opened possibilities of multicultural cooperation, to exclusionary national myths and scientific racism. And with the dampening of chances for war on the European continent itself, struggles shifted to competition for colonies overseas. Stronger central governments aided and benefited from the development of new technologies: the railroad and steamship, telegraphs, and artillery pieces that gave the European empires advantages in logistics and firepower over colonial resistance movements.

## 3 Asymmetry and Empires (1815–1914)

Despite the political challenges to the British and French Empires that proliferated during the Age of Revolutions, both systems proved their resiliency throughout the 19th century. The old empires of the North Atlantic gained in power despite the emergence of new imperial rivals in the United States and Germany by the end of the century. In this era of global imperial expansion, asymmetric conflicts of American Indian Removal took place alongside French and British wars in Africa, Asia, and Oceania. In each case, historians have debated the importance of settlers to empires of the era.

### 3.1 Settler Colonialism

Demography played variable roles for colonial populations. Malthusian fears of growing and desperate European underclasses found relief in imperial policies that encouraged settlement in overseas (or in the U.S. case, western overland) territories. The importance of civilian migrants varied among the empires. Even

---

[52] Robert R. Palmer, *The Age of the Democratic Revolution: A Political History of Europe and America, 1760-1800* (Princeton University Press, 2014), 792; David Bell, *Men on Horseback: The Power of Charisma in the Age of Revolution* (Picador, 2021).

within empires, some colonies possessed different amounts of political sway over home governments. Per historian James Belich, a crucial factor in the significance of settler populations to colonies was the initial presence of metropolitan women, who became "founding mothers."[53] For 19th-century British and American cases, large migrant populations weighed heavily on imperial policy. In the French case, until the end of the 19th century, it was the military instead that led the colonial effort.

Settlers sought indigenous peoples' land and had no use for their labor, unlike imperial agents of the military and trading companies in need of colonized peoples' cooperation. In places like Australia, where the British neglected to send regular troops for much of the colony's history (similar conditions existed in U.S. California and Oregon territories), settler colonialism has a great deal of explanatory power. In places like Florida, where federal military agents predominated over a weak territorial government, conditions do not follow the theory's logic as well.[54] In North Africa, which became integrated as French *départements* led by a military governor, and where settlers never became the dominant proportion of the population, the theory seems to explain still less.[55] Governments throughout the 19th-century Atlantic publicized their support to settlement from the metropole in order to distinguish their own allegedly virtuous colonization from previous efforts of extractive monarchical conquest. But cooperation between states and settlers within colonies was often aspirational rather than real, since the two groups had conflicts of interest with regard to exploitation versus elimination of indigenous peoples.

Many asymmetric aspects affected imperial wars of the 19th century, but factors of numerical strength and technology did not always favor the Euro-Americans. During the Second Seminole War (1835–1842), the United States deployed to Florida over 5,000 regular troops, or almost twice the total population of indigenous people who remained in the territory at the time. But the opposite situation applied for the British and French in Africa and Asia, where they confronted local governments with huge numerical advantages. In terms of technology, though the Seminoles lacked cannons and steamboats, trade relationships with the Spanish equipped them with rifles that matched

---

[53] James Belich, *Replenishing the Earth: The Settler Revolution and the Rise of the Angloworld* (Oxford University Press, 2011), 25–40, esp. 30, for global comparison of "settling societies." For more on settler colonialism, see Patrick Wolfe, *Settler Colonialism and the Transformation of Anthropology* (Cassell, 1999); Lorenzo Veracini, *Settler Colonialism: A Theoretical Overview* (Palgrave MacMillan, 2010).

[54] Walter Hixson, *American Settler Colonialism: A History* (Palgrave MacMillan, 2013), 63–85.

[55] Jennifer Sessions, *By Sword and Plow: France and the Conquest of Algeria* (Cornell University Press, 2011), 180–184; William Gallois, *A History of Violence in the Early Algerian Colony* (Palgrave Macmillan, 2013), 145–149.

contemporary U.S. army small arms.[56] During contemporary campaigns in India, Mughal and Sikh princes possessed heavy guns that outclassed those the British could carry with their formations. It was only at the end of this era that the Maxim gun, indirect-fire artillery, and (still later) airplanes provided clear advantages to imperial weaponry in the colonies.[57]

While numbers and weapons fluctuated in significance across imperial contexts, empires did maintain the strategic advantage of logistic resupply, now enhanced by new technologies of steam ships, railroads, and the telegraph. These innovations represented a broader trend of "scientific" warfare, a legacy of the polytechnic, engineering education that produced Napoleon and his generals, and which spread to the other Euro-American states in the generation that succeeded them.[58]

## 3.2 Wars of American Expansion

Science played a major role in American Indian Removal, a generations-long process. True, Jackson's operations in the Creek Civil War (1814) and the First Seminole War (1818–1819) had more to do with "First Way of War" attacks on crops and settlements than principles of contemporary science.[59] But the generation of regular officers who came of age during the War of 1812 often rejected Jackson's brand of fighting in favor of one that leveraged technology and diplomacy to minimize violence in Indian Country rather than escalate it.[60] This was the pattern in Florida, where regulars concentrated. But the U.S. army was tiny, no more than 12,000 soldiers total, in light of the continental scale of federal U.S. claims. As a result, endemic skirmishes took place between settlers and indigenous people in western territories, where regulars were mostly absent.

In Florida, the few settlers who migrated from the United States crowded into plantations in the northern third of the territory, leaving millions of acres of Everglades swamp to the indigenous resistance. During the Second Seminole

---

[56] John K. Mahon, *History of the Second Seminole War* (University Press of Florida, 1967), 120.

[57] Bruce Vandervort, *Indian Wars of Canada, Mexico, and the United States, 1812-1900* (Routledge, 2007), 101; Daniel Headrick, *The Tools of Empire: Technology and European Imperialism in the Nineteenth Century* (Oxford University Press, 1981).

[58] Ian Hope, *A Scientific Way of War: Antebellum Military Science, West Point, and the Origins of American Military Thought* (University of Nebraska Press, 2015); Sudhir Hazareesingh, *The Legend of Napoleon* (Granta, 2004).

[59] Grenier, *First Way of War,* 5–12; Robert Remini, *Andrew Jackson and His Indian Wars* (Viking, 2001).

[60] Samuel Watson, "Military Learning and Adaptation Shaped by Social Context: The US Army and Its 'Indian Wars,' 1790-1890," *Journal of Military History*, vol. 82, no. 2 (April 2018), 373–412, esp. 409–411; Watson, "How the Army Became Accepted: West Point Socialization, Military Accountability, and the Nation-State during the Jacksonian Era," *Nineteenth Century History*, vol. 7, no. 2, 219–251, esp. 231–2.

War (1835–1842), indigenous resistance fighters wielded an asymmetric advantage of intelligence about the local topography, which allowed them to evade U.S. patrols and choose the timing of the few battles of the war. Commanding General Thomas Jesup grew so frustrated with the perceived deceits of his enemies that he ordered subordinates to capture resistance leader Osceola under the false auspices of a "white flag" talk. The deceptive tactic became politicized, as Whig Party officials opposed to the reckless expansion of Jackson's faction used the incident to castigate the Democrats who ran the war. The unpopular conflict ended after seven years, even as several communities of Seminoles remained in Florida.[61]

The biggest tactical problem for U.S. agents during the war was one of mobility. American forces attempted to overcome their lack of speed through the creation of a regular cavalry unit, the importation of "bloodhound" dogs from Cuba, and the invention of an improvised explosive device (IED). This latter innovation was the product of infantry Captain Gabriel Rains, who built two prototypes out of howitzer shells, some powder and metal fragments, and old military uniforms to entice Native Americans to set off the detonator. The IED, like the bloodhounds satirized in Figure 3, failed to have any effect on the

**Figure 3** Napoleon Sarony, "Secretary of War presenting colors to a Regiment of Bloodhounds," 1840, Wikimedia Commons

---

[61] Daniel Howe, *What Hath God Wrought: The Transformation of America, 1815-1848* (Oxford University Press, 2007), 516–518.

course of the war, even at the tactical level, but these tactics demonstrated the range of adaptations, along with the steamboat, by which U.S. forces attempted to close the mobility gap.[62]

The Mexican-American War (1846–1848) arose over a boundary dispute in Texas, a former Mexican territory recently annexed by the United States. Though combatants from both republics fought campaigns on conventional lines, two important asymmetric aspects affected the contours of the war. First, U.S. armies that invaded Mexico found its northern territories depopulated by years of Comanche raids; local populations had become disillusioned with federal politicians in Mexico City as a result. Second, following defeat of its Mexican counterpart, the U.S. army attempted occupation of an extensive territory. General Winfield Scott, wary of recent Napoleonic troubles in Spain, developed what might be called the counterinsurgency playbook, as he advised subordinates to protect Mexican property, respect the Catholic Church, keep indigenous officials at their posts, reestablish public services such as schools and hospitals, and distribute rations to the poor. All of these efforts combined to marginalize insurgents.[63]

The Mexican War land cession provoked tensions on the issue of slavery that led to the American Civil War (1861–1865), another conflict in which guerrilla fighting constituted a significant aspect. As much as one third of the entire Union army had to garrison regions of questionable loyalty in Missouri, Kentucky, and Maryland. The rebels, too, struggled to deal with Unionist sabotage in much of Appalachia. The Confederate States of America (CSA) created light cavalry "Partisan Ranger" units, which raised their own recruits and supplies, lived among the people, and thus blurred the line between public service and criminality. The Union government adopted a legal code developed by Francis Lieber (1863) to define public warfare as fought between states and distinct from private war, waged by independent "bushwhackers" without official connection to a government and thus liable to summary execution rather than captivity as prisoners of war.[64]

The problems of distinguishing between the legitimate partisans and guerrillas, war-rebels, and other bushwhackers led some Union commanders to "hard war"

---

[62] Jacob Hagstrom, "'The Nature of Their Country': Florida's Environment and Military Learning in the Second Seminole War, 1835-1842," *Florida Historical Quarterly*, vol. 100, no. 3 (Winter 2022), 253–280, esp. 264–266.

[63] Brian DeLay, *War of a Thousand Deserts: Indian Raids and the US-Mexican War* (Yale University Press, 2008); Peter Guardino, *The Dead March: A History of the Mexican-American War* (Harvard University Press, 2017), 123–125, 295–297; Andrew J. Birtle, *U.S. Army Counterinsurgency and Contingency Operations Doctrine, 1860-1941*, vol. 1 (Center for Military History, 1998), 16–17.

[64] John Fabian Witt, *Lincoln's Code: The Law of War in American History* (Simon and Schuster, 2012).

policies: the execution of prisoners, deportation of rebellious populations, and destruction of private property. General William T. Sherman, a veteran of the Second Seminole War, used his forces to target the upper-class slaveholders who had led the secession movement. Other Union officers created specialized counterguerrilla units that emphasized the collection of local intelligence, rapid movement including by night, and ambush tactics. Insurgency continued during the Union's occupation of the defeated CSA during the years of Reconstruction, though usually to enforce a race-based social code rather than to challenge the political reintegration of the states into the Union.[65]

## 3.3 France and North Africa

The U.S. military of the early 19th century reached out to learn from the French, who were engaged in their own war of southern expansion in North Africa. Political theorist Alexis de Tocqueville, among others, argued the only way to "win" a colonial war was to export masses of settlers from France. But Algeria, like Florida, proved an unpopular place for metropolitan migrants. French commander Thomas-Robert Bugeaud proposed to wage war by "sword and plow," with the creation of military colonies adjacent to settlers, to be led by veterans after their periods of service in Africa. These experiments tended to fail in practice, and the French government abandoned the interior of the colony for long periods through the 1830s and 1840s to hole up in coastal enclaves.[66]

Abd el Kader, the most effective leader of North African resistance, learned to incorporate more conventional elements of combat as the years of conflict passed. Unlike Osceola in Florida, who led perhaps a few hundred soldiers at the height of his rebellion, Abd el Kader led thousands of infantrymen organized into battalions, recruited tens of thousands more cavalrymen through tribal militia, and even culled French deserters into specialized units of engineering, logistics, and artillery. But like Osceola and his traditionalist, anti-imperial religious rhetoric, the "iron Emir" was a master of political action. In North Africa, the call to *jihad* had been well rehearsed, but Abd el Kader further benefited from recent examples of French atrocity to persuade locals to aid his troops and turn their backs on the wealthy *sheiks* of the colonial administration. French General Bugeaud's war of conquest in Algeria, like Jesup's in Florida, was a stop-and-start affair, marked by episodes of atrocity alongside those of negotiation. French colonial historians have described separate phases of assimilation, association, and extermination in discrete periods, but military

---

[65] Brian McKnight and Barton Myers, eds., *The Guerrilla Hunters: Irregular Conflicts during the Civil War* (Louisiana State University Press, 2017).
[66] Sessions, *Sword and Plow*, 2–6, 205.

records reveal that all three modes occurred throughout the French colonial era. Local conditions in Africa had more of an effect on the likelihood of French atrocities at any given time than did policies from Paris.[67]

Historians have singled out Bugeaud as a special proponent of *razzia*, raids on indigenous settlements and herds, but his predecessors in command had not hesitated to order these practices, as well. What separated Bugeaud from the other commanders was his outspokenness in the press and his self-promotion as a military innovator. Bugeaud's reforms in Algeria were operational rather than cultural. He counseled subordinates to create "flying columns" without heavy guns and baggage, but he had little effect on mindsets within the *Armée d'Afrique*, which was already an aggressive and unruly force by the late 1830s. The difference between fighting in Europe and Africa, in Bugeaud's mind, had less to do with the humanity of his opponents, and more with divergent centers of gravity. In Europe, these comprised large military units and towns, whereas in North Africa, herds and crops became primary targets. On both continents, French commanders engaged noncombatants with violence when they interfered with the safety or political ends of occupying military forces. After all, Bugeaud and his generation of French officers had been introduced to warfare through sieges and bombardments against Spanish settlements suspected of harboring *guerrillas*.[68]

## 3.4 Britain and South Africa

General Harry Smith, like Andrew Jackson and Thomas-Robert Bugeaud, began his military career during the Napoleonic Era. He contrasted his experiences in America, which he denigrated as "milito-nautico-guerrilla-plundering warfare," with examples of "humane warfare" under the Duke of Wellington against France. Smith was disturbed by orders to burn the American capital, a practice which he claimed to be suitable only for Native American warfare. After this unsettling debut, Smith went on to fight in India and South Africa.[69]

---

[67] Osama Abi-Mershed, *Apostles of Modernity: Saint Simonians and the Civilizing Mission in Algeria* (Stanford University Press, 2010), 4–9; Charles-Andre Julien, *Histoire de l'Algerie Contemporaine: La Conquete et les Debuts de la Colonisation 1827-1871* (Presses Universitaires de France, 1964), 182.

[68] Douglas Porch, "Bugeaud, Gallieni, Lyautey: The Development of French Colonial Warfare," in Peter Paret, ed. *Makers of Modern Strategy* (Princeton University Press, 1986), 378–380; Sessions, *Sword and Plow*, 162–163; Jacob Hagstrom, "'My Soldiers Above All': Justifying Violence against Noncombatants in French Algeria, 1830-1847, "*Journal of Military History*, vol. 86, no. 1 (January 2022), 32–53, esp. 45–46.

[69] G. C. Moore Smith, ed., *The Autobiography of Sir Harry Smith, 1787-1819* (London: J. Murray, 1910), 200 1, 240, 248, 251; *The War in India: Despatches of the Right Honourable Lt. Gen. Viscount Hardinge, General Lord Gough, and Maj. Gen. Sir Harry Smith* (London: John Ollivier, 1846), 57–63.

Though the Indian campaigns took place between two professional armies, each equipped with cavalry and artillery, the British Xhosa Wars (1811–1879) of South Africa were interminable conflicts of rebellion and counterinsurgency, periods of diplomacy interrupted by massacres, much like the American wars of Indian Removal and the French conquest of North Africa.

Wars of the Cape began with British attempts to protect shipping to India around the time of the French Revolution. The first attempts at settlement began only later, in 1820. The correspondence of British imperial officials reveals that they used the defense of settlers as a mere excuse for their true purposes: to gain more resources from London and extend their mandates over indigenous land.[70] Settlers' critiques of indigenous Africans focused on economic aspects of property and labor; descriptors such as "theivish" and "indolent" are rife in their communications. But military officers' criticisms of indigenous people as ungovernable, "treacherous" or "barbaric," proved more alarming in London. British military officials succeeded in growing their power relative to civil authorities through calls to war. Fewer than 2,000 British regulars took part in the Sixth War during the mid-1830s, which Smith waged as military commander against one Xhosa king. During the Eighth War of the 1850s, Smith oversaw 8,000 regular soldiers as military governor, as they countered a more general rebellion in the newly established territory of British Kaffiria. The British in South Africa relied on well-established tropes of "savagery" to undermine the authority of indigenous leaders and justify colonial dispossession.[71]

The British used a divide-and-conquer strategy to augment their numbers and close the intelligence gap with indigenous people, as did the Americans across the Atlantic. In Florida, U.S. commanders employed liberty diplomacy to attract Black Seminoles, people who had escaped slavery and lived among the Seminoles, to serve as interpreters, guides, and porters for the army in exchange for resettlement as freemen in the West.[72] In South Africa, British leaders encouraged the defection of the minority Fingo people to scout rebel positions, in some cases to serve as a "decoy" to draw out potential ambushers. Not only did the British consider Fingo fighters more expendable, but indigenous allies required no cash as colonial troops did, since they accepted captured cattle and other plunder as compensation. Moreover, British officials assessed that the Fingo

---

[70] Stephen M. Miller, ed., *Soldiers and Settlers in Africa, 1850-1918* (Brill, 2009), 2.

[71] Jochen Arndt, "Treacherous Savages and Merciless Barbarians: Knowledge, Discourse and Violence during the Cape Frontier Wars, 1834-1853," *Journal of Military History*, vol. 74, no. 3 (July 2010), 709–735, esp. 714.

[72] Kevin Mulroy, *The Seminole Freedmen: A History* (University of Oklahoma Press, 2007), 48–51.

people were accustomed to the kind of scorched-earth tactics they sought to employ, though Britons proved they, too, could employ harsh measures.[73]

## 3.5 Russia and Central Asia

For centuries, the Russian empire maintained a consistent southern border that stretched eastward from the Caspian Sea. But from the 1830s until the end of the century, the Tsarist government expanded to include 1.5 million square miles of territory in Central Asia and more than 6 million new subjects, almost all of whom practiced the Muslim faith. Why did the Russians expand so rapidly? British observers often answered by pointing to the "natural" aggression of their imperial opponents. Russian historians, on the other hand, described the economic resources that pulled the empire further south. The most recent scholarly works on the topic, however, reject any overarching political or economic "grand strategy" in favor of the complex interactions between officials in St. Petersburg, ambitious Russian agents "on the spot," Central Asian rulers, and "disobedient" local peoples.[74]

The Russian army benefited from a near-monopoly on infantry and artillery forces in the region throughout the decades of conquest. Their problems against indigenous irregular cavalry, which resembled the Russians' own Cossacks, were more logistical than tactical. Massive convoys of camels perished during attempts to cross the vast deserts of the region. The Russians, through a series of sieges on cities and fortresses, kept their own casualties remarkably low. One contemporary historian recorded the total killed and wounded from 1853 to 1881 in Central Asia at just over 3,000, or fewer than the Russian losses in one day at the battle of the Alma River during the Crimean War.

Operations in the Semirechye (Jetisu) region exhibited parallels with the contemporaneous French campaigns in North Africa. Both conquests began with small-scale operations against raiders on the territory of an indigenous Muslim Empire. Whereas the French in North Africa undercut Ottoman authorities, the Russians in Semirechye contested the Kokand Khanate's claims to authority over restive Kazakh and Kyrgyz nobles. The Russian analog to the French Bugeaud was General Gerasim Kolpakovskii, who began his career in the enlisted ranks and crushed a revolt in Europe before his deployment to the Ala-Tau region. Kolpakovskii, like Bugeaud, sought to secure military gains

---

[73] Tim Stapleton, "'Valuable, Gallant and Faithful Assistants': The Fingo (or Mfengu) as Colonial Military Allies" in Miller, ed., *Soldiers and Settlers*, 18, 46–47.

[74] Alexander Morrison, *The Russian Conquest of Central Asia: A Study in Imperial Expansion, 1814-1914* (Cambridge University Press, 2022), 9–10, 20–24; Bruce Menning, *Bayonets before Bullets: The Russian Army, 1861-1914* (Indiana University Press, 2000); Alex Marshall, *The Russian General Staff and Asia, 1860-1917* (Routledge, 2006).

with the importation of settlers and crops from Europe. These Russian experiments, as with the French ones, resulted in little migration until the region's connection to Russia's network of railroads. The site of the city Almaty comprised a sparse military fortification for decades before it finally cultivated a population of more than 20,000 by the end of the 19th century.[75]

One of the region's most significant and mythologized campaigns was the Russian occupation of Tashkent. In June 1865, General Mikhail G. Chernyaev led a force of fewer than 2,000 men to take the largest city of the region, populated by more than 100,000, with a loss of just 25 soldiers killed. The event was typical of the "disobedience" thesis of Russian military history, in which bureaucrats issued vague or contradicting orders but accepted the successes of "rogue generals" in the field. Recent research argues that the Russian metropolitan elites may have disagreed with the timing of Chernyaev's actions, and they disdained his initial failure to take the city, but their goals for Russian expansion aligned with those of the man on the spot. Chernyaev was sensitive to the cultural differences of the newest Russian subjects, as he worked through the local *ulama* to ensure post-battle administration and to reassure the people of Tashkent that their religious values were safe under Russian patronage. His actions indicated contrasting motivations for Russians in Central Asia, as they claimed to "civilize" indigenous inhabitants, while at the same time governing with as light a touch as possible.[76]

The Russians, along with the other European empires, committed atrocities during their imperial campaigns. Transcaspia, in the borderlands of Qajar Persia, became the particular subject of international scandal due to the leadership of General Mikhail Skobelev, whom even a reserved historian of Russia labeled a "revolting sadist." After a brutal "pacification" campaign in Ferghana in 1875–1876, Skobelev encouraged the massacre of 8,000 Turkmen, including many women and children, during their attempts to flee the fortress of Goek Tepe in January 1881. Yet historian Alexander Morrison concludes that Skobelev's leadership alone cannot explain the growing tendency of Russians to massacre the inhabitants of the cities they conquered toward the end of the 19th century, as the forces became more asymmetric over time. Morrison suggests some "clear parallels" to the conditions of French Algeria in the 19th century, as he notes, "the reputation shared by Turkmen and the Touareg for savagery, insolence, and slave-raiding," which drew the disgust and extreme violence of invading European soldiers. In most places, there was little resistance to the Russian Empire after its initial conquest, as local leaders retained their administrative roles and the Russians contented themselves with more or less indirect rule. Only 30,000 imperial troops

---

[75] Morrison, *Russian Conquest*, 30–48, 168–190.

[76] Morrison, *Russian Conquest*, 217, 237, 250–252; see also David MacKenzie, *The Lion of Tashkent: The Career of General M.G. Cherniaev* (University of Georgia Press, 1974).

administered the entire region in the last decades of the 19th century. Violence did not arrive for most Central Asian peoples until European settlement accelerated in the early 20th century, following the revolt of the summer of 1916.[77]

## 3.6 French "Civilizing Missions"

As the 19th century turned into the 20th, European empires began to revise the logic for their military affairs. Imperialists started to justify their campaigns by pointing to alleged benefits of their system for the people of the colonies, themselves, as they added to older arguments about economics or the glory of the metropole. The French use of the term *mission civilisatrice* dated to 1840, a few years before the American term "Manifest Destiny" appeared. In the French case, a contributor to the Geographic Society posited, "Expatriation is an economic need, a political necessity, a civilizing progress."[78] Though French observers often contrasted their universalist assimilation project as distinct from the Anglo-Saxon methods of expulsion and extermination, in practice all imperial campaigns contained a chaotic mix of cultural attraction and economic opportunity, backed by ready resorts to violence.

French Generals Joseph Gallieni and Hubert Lyautey became preeminent theorists of counterinsurgency warfare. They sought to reframe colonial war at the end of the 19th century as a beneficent enterprise, rather than the brute conquest of previous generations. The officers coined the phrase "hearts and minds" to describe the project of political and economic suasion that they practiced in Indochina to prevent atrocities and minimize local resistance to the French Empire.[79] Lyautey summarized their approach:

- Diplomacy and political settlements took precedence over military operations.
- Columns of troops gave way to a "creeping occupation," in the *tache d'huile* (oil stain) method.
- Military occupation encouraged economic development, which resulted in political stability.

Lyautey advocated these principles be implemented by a unified command, under the authority of one professional soldier.[80] Thus, for all the apparent reforms to

---

[77] Morrison, *Russian Conquest*, 409–411, 535–539.

[78] S. Dutot, *De L'Expatriation* (Arthus Bertrand, 1840), 320–321; Sessions, *Sword and Plow*, p. 6; for "Manifest Destiny," see John O'Sullivan, "Annexation," *The United States Magazine and Democratic Review*, vol. 17 (1845), 5–10.

[79] Porch, "Bugeaud, Gallieni, Lyautey," 392–393.

[80] Hubert Lyautey, "Du Role Sociale de l'officier dans le service militare universelle," *Revue des Deux Mondes*, 15 March 1891, 443–459; Lyautey, "Du Role Colonial de l'Armée," *Revue des Deux Mondes*, 15 January 1900, 308–328.

the French conduct of colonial warfare, decision-making concentrated in an autocrat, who was free to combine harsh and conciliatory tactics as he saw fit, much as predecessors had done in previous campaigns. French officers assumed offensive operations to be necessary at the outset of pacification, to clear out armed resistance before less violent and more productive phases could follow.[81] The second wave of French colonial operations expanded the claims of empire from North Africa to West Africa, Madagascar, and Southeast Asia.

The British, not to be outdone by their continental rivals, intensified their own efforts in Africa. By the eve of the First World War, London had directed offensives throughout the eastern part of the continent, north from its Cape Colony and south from Egypt. Britons drew newfound confidence from technological tools with applications to warfare, with the "machine gun" as the most iconic and aptly named among a host of industrial inventions: indirect-fire artillery, poison gas, and airplanes.[82] These innovations made strong European powers stronger still in terms of military power projection, just as they sought to adopt softer, more benevolent rhetoric.

## 3.7 The Dutch in Indonesia

The Dutch, like the Russians and French, listed prestige of state and pride of culture as reasons to justify a growing colonial realm. Unlike those other European empires, concerned to keep up with British rivals, the Dutch relied on the British navy for protection. The Netherlands had deep historical connections to Java, the most populous of the Indonesian islands, through the spice-trading activity of its East India Company. The official government policy was not to occupy new territories from the Javan base, but to encourage company officials to sign contracts with surrounding indigenous sultanates. In 1841, the minister of colonies even ordered a retreat from new posts in Sumatra.

Government policy changed after the massacres at Lombok in 1894 and subsequent Dutch military campaigns in Aceh, 1896–1898. Afterward, the Dutch began direct political expansion into the "outer regions." As with the Russians in Central Asia, there was no "conspiracy" from Europe to annex the entire archipelago. Instead, local agents tended to make requests to the colonial Indies government, rather than wait for instructions from the Netherlands. The process developed into a feedback loop, according to historian Elsbeth Locher-Scholten, in which "Dutch demands and pressure" for more political and

---

[81] Michael Finch, *A Progressive Occupation: The Gallieni-Lyautey Method and Colonial Pacification in Tonkin and Madagascar, 1885-1900* (Oxford University Press, 2013), 1–5; Barnett Singer and John Langdon, *Cultured Force: Makers and Defenders of the French Colonial Empire* (University of Wisconsin Press, 2004).

[82] John Ellis, *The Social History of the Machine Gun* (Johns Hopkins University Press, 1986).

economic control resulted in "growing Indonesian opposition," which officials addressed with more demands for military campaigns. The leader of those efforts was General J.B. Van Heutsz, who developed what he called the Aceh strategy: "use of a mobile military police force, trained in guerrilla warfare, and the temporary concentration of military and civil authority." The formula was similar to the one developed by French theorists Lyautey and Gallieni.

Dutch government authorities conceived of their expansion throughout the Indonesian archipelago as an "Ethical Policy" as of 1901. The high-mindedness from Europe did not prevent atrocities by military forces. Instead, the policy forced colonial officials to find pretexts of local grievance with indigenous leaders before they could intervene on behalf of the population. This was easy to do given the sultans' "excesses" of luxury from the perspectives of "Calvinist mentality" Dutch agents. The shift from indirect trade partnership to direct political control was more the result of bureaucracy than it was a question of morality or even economics. The systematic control that some administrators had sought since the first half of the century became feasible once technical logistical problems decreased. The pathway to more formal empire opened with the founding of the national shipping company KPM in 1888. All that remained afterward was for local entrepreneurs to ask for the resources to expand their purviews. These demands became urgent after 1894, as the first Japanese war for control over the Korean Peninsula signaled a new entrant to the global imperialist competition.[83]

## 3.8 The United States and the Philippines

When crisis in Cuba lent an excuse to declare war, American imperialists took advantage of an overextended Spanish empire. The humanitarian rationale, to assist rebels against cruel Spanish colonizers, provided cover for American agents' desires for tropical resources, markets of consumers, and overseas ports for the growing naval power. Mere hours after the sinking of the *USS Maine* in Havana harbor in February 1898, the U.S. Navy destroyed the Spanish fleet that defended the capital of the Philippines in Manila. While the conventional war with Spain lasted only until August and cost the lives of 379 American soldiers and sailors, the counterinsurgency against Filipino revolutionaries dragged on across four years, during which 4,000 American servicemen died, along with 16,000 Filipino fighters and hundreds of thousands more noncombatants.

---

[83] Elsbeth Locher-Scholten, "Dutch Expansion in the Indonesian Archipelago around 1900 and the Imperialism Debate," *Journal of Southeast Asian Studies*, vol. 25, no. 1 (March 1994), 91–111; see also Thijs W. Brocades Zaalberg, "The Roots of Dutch Counterinsurgency: Balancing and Integrating Military and Civilian Efforts from Aceh to Uruzgan," ed. Richard G Davis, *The U.S. Army and Irregular Warfare, 1775-2007* (Center for Military History, 2008), 119–132.

When the U.S. government resolved to keep the Philippines and its seven million inhabitants, President William McKinley claimed that he acted "to educate the Filipinos, and uplift and Christianize them."[84] Such lofty idealism belied the terror and torture that Americans used to conquer their new colony. In many ways, military operations continued much as they had over the previous generation in the American West. In the fall of 1899, one general officer opined: "Filipinos are in identically the same position as the Indians of our country have been for many years, and must be subdued in much the same way, by such convincing conquest as shall make them realize fully the futility of armed resistance, and then win them by fair and just treatment."[85] Most senior army leaders had experience fighting Native Americans, and they applied this Indian Country template of overwhelming violence at the outset of the campaign, followed by the establishment of a police state, abetted by indigenous allies.

Operations alongside Filipino auxiliaries brought U.S. agents both opportunity and risk. General Frederick Funston was wary about the reaction from Washington after he used Macabebe scouts to trick resistance leader Emilio Aguinaldo into captivity in 1901. Though Funston understood the tactic was deceptive, he concluded that no other method would be as expedient. Similar logic justified the use of torture to extract intelligence from prisoners. During interrogation, U.S. soldiers and their indigenous allies pinned captives to the ground, fixed sticks in their mouths, and poured water down their throats until they "swell[ed] up like toads," as shown in Figure 4. It was not what the American public had come to expect from a "civilizing mission." Moreover, torture to extort confessions had been forbidden by paragraph 16 of the Lieber Code (1863). The "water cure" was only one of the harsh techniques that the United States directed against Aguinaldo's resistance movement. Americans burned crops and villages in an attempt to force populations out of enemy-controlled regions and "concentrate" them close to military outposts. The worst of the abuses took place on the island of Samar, where General Jacob Smith gave orders to his subordinates to turn the surrounding territory into a "howling wilderness."[86]

---

[84] Aaron B. O'Connell, "Defending Imperial Interests in Asia and the Caribbean," in James Bradford, ed. *America, Sea Power, and the World* (Wiley, 2016), 150–164.

[85] Cited in Birtle, vol. 1, 112.

[86] Frederick Funston, *Memories of Two Wars: Cuban and Philippine Experiences* (Scribner, 1911), 384–426; Richard Welch, "American Atrocities in the Philippines: The Indictment and the Response," *Pacific Historical Review*, vol. 43 (1974), 233–253, esp. 235–236; Glenn May, *The Battle for Batangas* (Yale University Press, 1991), 257–262; Brian Linn, *The Philippine War, 1899-1902* (University of Kansas Press, 2000), 308–316.

**Figure 4** The water cure on the cover of *Life Magazine*, May 22, 1902, Wikimedia Commons

Along with attempts to "chastise" rebellious Filipinos, some U.S. officers employed the pacification policy of "attraction." Americans built roads and protected markets in efforts to court the population, more focused on survival than politics. U.S. agents believed education to be a generational solution to the cultural problems that they faced with their new colonial charges. By the end of 1900, the army built more than 1,000 schools and dispensed patronage in an attempt to forge a new indigenous elite amenable to American concepts of governance and economy.[87]

Though top-level commanders often talked the talk of attraction, the actions of subordinates suggested a preference for punitive measures. One veteran officer who began the war as an enthusiastic proponent of education reform and general goodwill concluded that in the end the Filipinos were motivated "by fear more than by any other impulse." The United States continued to concentrate populations of rebel-held regions and remained aggressive after the official end of the war in 1902 on the southern islands of Mindanao, where operations against rebellious Muslim Moro *datos* entailed the use of artillery for the destruction of homes and raids by Provisional Companies, elite units of men who had completed a qualification course that included marksmanship, first aid, and swimming with equipment.[88]

The worst atrocity of the era took place in March 1906, under the command of General Leonard Wood. U.S. troops, most of them regular soldiers of the 6th infantry and the 4th cavalry, slaughtered more than 900 men, women, and children who had taken refuge in the crater of Bud Dajo. The incident was exceptional, and not only for its taking place after official military campaigns had concluded – the timing allowed for U.S. authorities to frame the victims as "bandits" and worse, rather than enemy combatants. This group of rebels had fled to the mountain to avoid new taxes of the colonial authorities, which alienated much of the local *dato* leadership. Some historians have analyzed this incident, the atrocities in Samar, and the war as a whole through the anachronistic lens of prehistory for the My Lai incident during the Vietnam War. This interpretation traces a special path to atrocity for the United States that counteracts outdated narratives of American exceptionalism. But this new focus on massacres, logics of "extermination," and the attendant insistence on moralizing, makes for as poor an historical premise as those that obscure violence in order to celebrate military agents or events.[89]

Most Americans in the Philippines, as during the previous Civil War–era generation, recognized that some combination of "benevolence and retaliation," fairness but firmness, was required to implement more intensive forms of government and subdue the insurrections that emerged. Historian Brian Linn

---

[87] Birtle, vol. 1, 121; John M. Gates, *Schoolbooks and Krags: The U.S. Army in the Philippines, 1898-1902* (Greenwood Press, 1973).

[88] Quote cited in Birtle, vol. 1, 127; see also Birtle, vol. 1, 166.

[89] Kim Wagner, *Massacre in the Clouds: An American Atrocity and the Erasure of History* (Public Affairs, 2024), see esp. "Conclusion" for comparisons to Vietnam; for more on the concept of race war, see Paul Kramer, *Blood of Government: Race, Empire, the United States, and the Philippines* (University of North Carolina Press, 2006), 146–153; Oliver Charbonneau, *Civilizational Imperatives: Americans, Moros, and the Colonial World* (Cornell University Press, 2020).

has suggested the major campaigns of the war and its outcome had little to do with atrocities. Instead, the war had been Aguinaldo's loss, and victory fell to the Americans by default. The rebel leader's brand of nationalism failed to attract many adherents beyond a small clique of Tagalog oligarchs on Luzon island, and resistance to empire, in most places throughout the islands, was muted.[90] The Philippines became the largest and most populous American acquisition in a larger colonial project that included Guam, Hawaii, and Cuba, each occupied in a similar pattern by veterans of the Indian Wars, with intelligence and manpower supplied by indigenous sources.[91]

## 3.9 Colonial Warfare and Counterinsurgency in Europe

In 1899, when British army officer Charles Callwell wrote the preface to the second edition of his popular *Small Wars*, he took note of the ongoing American campaigns in the Philippines, along with the French presence in Madagascar, and the British in Sudan, Rhodesia, and the Northwest Indian frontier. The British Empire was then months away from yet another colonial war against the Boers, which bolstered global interest in Callwell's topic and inspired a third edition in 1906. By then, the volume included the author's experience as staff officer and field commander in South Africa. Over the past century, many writers have cited the text in their analyses of asymmetric conflicts around the world.[92]

Callwell began his work by recognizing the limits of his descriptor, "small." The term, he admitted, "has in reality no particular connection with the scale" of the conflicts, but instead referred to the asymmetry of the forces that opposed colonization. With language typical of the age, Callwell specified his subject as, "expeditions against savages and semi-civilized races by disciplined soldiers." He believed the psychological effect of imperial campaigns, based on "bold initiative and resolute action," was essential for "overawing" indigenous peoples, to enable long term stability.[93] In recent decades, Callwell has attracted

---

[90] Linn, *Philippine War*, 323–324.

[91] David Silbey, *A War of Frontier and Empire: The Philippine-American War 1899-1902* (Hill and Wang, 2007); Katherine Bjork, *Prairie Imperialists: The Indian Country Origins of American Empire* (University of Pennsylvania Press, 2019).

[92] The USMC Small Wars Doctrine (1940) does not cite Callwell, though it is patently derivative, 1-2; see also Douglas Porch, "Introduction," Charles Edward Callwell, *Small Wars: Their Principles and Practice* (University of Nebraska Press, 1996); for other applications in recent doctrine, see FM 3–24: Counterinsurgency (University of Chicago Press, 2007), 391; Gavin Bulloch, *Countering Insurgency, British Army Field Manual*, vol. 1, part 10 (2009), 1–1; MAJ John Sullivan, "The Marine Corps Small Wars Manual and Colonel C. E. Callwell's Small Wars: Relevant to the Twenty-First Century or Anachronisms?" *Small Wars Journal*, vol. 2, no. 3 (2006), 71–90.

[93] Charles Edward Callwell, *Small Wars: Their Principles and Practice* (Harrison and Sons, 1906), 21, 24.

criticism for these racist premises. Historian Douglas Porch, for example, branded modern counterinsurgency theory as "deceptive marketing," designed to placate imperial home fronts with promises of "small" campaigns while their militaries sallied forth to "protracted, unlimited, murderous, expensive, total-war assaults on indigenous societies." According to critics of counterinsurgency, present-day practitioners have attempted to use the imperial British military thinker to grant asymmetric warfare a more respectable pedigree than it deserves.[94]

While some scholars labeled Callwell the father of counterinsurgency doctrine, for good or for ill, he need not be pigeonholed as such. In addition to *Small Wars*, Callwell published another major work, *Military Operations and Maritime Preponderance* (1905). Consideration of the two works together complicates Callwell's status as a special prophet of modern counterinsurgency; his views on colonial wars are inseparable from the broader geopolitical issues of his era. At the turn of the 20th century, global naval power consisted of a hegemonic British force and a series of weaker competitors, who sought to use the emergent technology of the torpedo and the employment of interservice amphibious operations to compete.[95] In particular, the rising challenges of the Germans and the Japanese to the British navy drove interstate conflict over the course of the subsequent decades and resulted in a new wave of asymmetric warfare in the context of two world wars.

Another link between colonial and interstate warfare consisted of imperial techniques imported to Europe. Some historians of Germany have claimed that colonial experiences provided the mindset and the techniques that help explain the ready resort to violence against noncombatants in Europe during the world wars. Others have argued for an older German way of war, a *Sonderweg* that was already evident in the struggle against French citizen-soldier militias, before the establishment of the German colonies in Africa.[96]

During the Franco-Prussian War (1870–1871), *Francs-tireurs* (free shooters) comprised small groups of civilians, deserters, and survivors of surrendered units who took up arms against the invading Germans after the abdication of Napoleon III in early September 1870. The new republican government in France, hearkening back to the revolutionary era, encouraged a *levée en masse* (rising altogether)

---

[94] Daniel Whittingham, *Charles E. Callwell and the British Way in Warfare* (Cambridge University Press, 2020), 9–10.

[95] Katherine Epstein, *Torpedo: Inventing the Military-Industrial Complex in the United States and Great Britain* (Harvard University Press, 2014).

[96] Isabel Hull, *Absolute Destruction: Military Practices and the Culture of War in Imperial Germany* (Cornell University Press, 2005), 3; Bastian Matteo Scianna, "A Predisposition to Brutality? German practices against civilians and francs-tireurs," *Small Wars and Insurgencies*, vol. 20, no. 5, 968–993.

to defend the homeland. For Germans, however, the appearance of *francs-tireurs* threatened to annul their battlefield victories and indicated a breakdown in the order of society. Chancellor Otto von Bismarck called for, and some commanders issued, stark reprisals on towns where their soldiers had been fired upon or otherwise sabotaged. The most common method of revenge was the mild means of tax compensation from offending towns. In other cases, German forces took local notables hostage during occupation. In a few instances, the Germans retaliated by rounding up and executing French men.[97]

Some historians claimed that memories of the *francs-tireurs*, rather than colonial experiences in Africa, drove the German atrocities in Belgium and northern France during the first months of the First World War, as soldiers sought to nip the possibility of a people's war in the bud.[98] Others countered that the French insurgency of 1870, as well as German countermeasures, has been exaggerated in the historical record. There were no more than 57,000 *francs-tireurs* in the field throughout the Franco-Prussian War; the amateur fighters made a limited mark on operations and caused no more than 1,000 of the Germans' 28,000 battle deaths. Both the French, for the patriotic narrative of resistance, and the Germans, to criticize the chaotic republicanism of their enemy, had motivations to spread stories about the *francs-tireurs*. But in practice, the emergence of ad hoc citizen-soldiers during the war brought little of the "absolute destruction" that typified later campaigns in Germany's African colonies.[99]

In both Europe and the United States, irregular fighters proved less significant for their military contributions than for the political reactions they provoked. The prospect of urban fighting between soldiers, ad hoc militias, and civilians represented a nightmare situation for governments at war. Justification for "hard war" practices in the Union and German armies, and attempts to create a legal framework for irregular combatants, gained momentum in the 19th century before they came to the forefront during the world wars of the 20th century. Service by colonial subjects in the First World War (1914–1918) resulted not only in tactical and technical experiences, but in political awakenings as well. Rising literacy and the spread of radio broadcasting brought growing awareness

---

[97] Sibylle Scheipers, *Unlawful Combatants: a Genealogy of the Irregular Fighter* (Oxford University Press, 2015), 88–92; Geoffrey Wawro, *The Franco-Prussian War* (Cambridge University Press, 1995), 279.

[98] John Horne and Alan Kramer, *German Atrocities, 1914: A History of Denial* (Yale University Press, 2002); Jeff Lipkes, *Rehearsals: The German Army in Belgium, August 1914* (Leuven University Press, 2007).

[99] Michael Howard, *The Franco-Prussian War* (Rupert Hart-Davis, 1961), 252; Scianna, "Predisposition to Brutality," 977; Sanford Kanter, "Exposing the Myth of the Franco-Prussian War," *War and Society*, vol. 4, no. 1 (1986), 13–30, here 15; Hull, *Absolute Destruction*, 117–130.

of Euro-American abuses in their colonies, and with this consciousness came more support for local resistance movements.

## 4 Asymmetry and Global Wars (1914–1950)

The world wars produced the largest conventional battles yet seen alongside many examples of partisan campaigns and popular rebellions. Technology played a significant role in transforming the nature of combat in the 20th century, as gas, tanks, airplanes, rockets, and nuclear weapons demonstrated the growing military power of industrial states. Though atomic power came to dominate theoretical studies of war after the Second World War, the more significant technological development in practice was the mass production of automatic rifles such as the AK-47, the reliability and efficiency of which made untrained irregular fighters far more lethal than they had been with single shot firearms, as in the past.[100]

The two brief periods of global interstate violence did not settle political problems in a definitive manner, but instead gave way to a plethora of local armed conflicts. After the First World War, anti-imperial fighting erupted in Ireland, Ethiopia, and the Middle East mandates. After the Second World War, coalitions in China, Greece, the Philippines, and elsewhere that had come together to fight foreign occupations turned inward on each other. The United States sent aid and advisors to the anti-communist forces in these civil wars, which gave the conflicts their asymmetric character.

## 4.1 The United States and the Caribbean

U.S. interventions in the Caribbean continued throughout the era of the world wars. Frequent operations aided those Latin American governments which supported the interests of international capital. Observers began to deride the Marine Corps as "State Department troops" for their tendency to deploy in support of stability operations to promote the election or maintenance in power of pro-U.S. candidates.[101] The basis for intervention was President Theodore Roosevelt's corollary to the Monroe Doctrine. Not only should Europeans stay out of the Americas, according to Roosevelt, but the United States would take on the new role of hemispheric policeman. In a candid commentary on the "banana wars" of the interwar period, Marine General Smedley Butler, a two-time Medal

---

[100] Terry Kahaner, *AK-47: The Weapon that Changed the Face of War* (Wiley, 2007); Victor Davis Hanson, "The World's Most Popular Gun: The Long Road to the AK-47," *The New Atlantis* (Summer, 2011), 140–147; noted the ubiquity of the AK-47, with over 75 million produced, compared to just 8 million M-16s, 144.

[101] Birtle, vol. 1. 182; Allan Millett, *Semper Fidelis: The History of the USMC* (Macmillan, 1980), 150, 164, 174, 261.

of Honor winner, quipped that most of his thirty-three years in service had been spent "as a high class muscle man for big business, for Wall Street, and for the bankers; I was a racketeer, a gangster for capitalism … I might have given Al Capone a few hints. The best he could do was to operate his racket in three districts. I operated on three continents."[102] Butler's disillusionment with the American turn to chronic imperial warfare sounded a lonely warning, as he was drowned out by those who benefited from military interventions in the interests of commerce.

The U.S. military retained its presence on Cuba following the Spanish-American War of 1898. Unlike the occupations of Guam, Hawaii, the Philippines, and Puerto Rico, that of Cuba did not result in formal annexation. Congress forbade the absorption of the island (due to qualms about its racial makeup) with the Platt Amendment of 1902, which allowed the navy to keep bases on the island. Cuban veterans of the 1898 war staged a rebellion against their new government in 1906, which prompted a second U.S. campaign from 1906 to 1909. Civilian and military authorities, as in the Philippines, promoted a program of nation building to attract the masses along with armed patrols against resistant holdouts. As development projects took shape, the U.S. military established a robust system of local informants, as each district formed its own intelligence service. Once U.S. officers had an understanding of local conditions, they set about to separate the population from insurgents through forced concentration and crop destruction. After the populace was under surveillance, the U.S. military and Cuban Rural Guards auxiliaries swept through the countryside.[103]

The reforms that the United States imposed on Cuba reinforced predatory economic conditions on the island. Ongoing political instability prompted new U.S. military interventions in 1912 and from 1917 to 1922. In the interwar period, the Americans backed the military junta that installed Fulgencio Batista. By the end of his reign in the late 1950s, U.S. companies owned all of the oil, 90 percent of electrical services, 90 percent of the mines, and almost half of the island's robust sugar production.[104] Cuba was only one site of the banana wars, which proceeded elsewhere in Costa Rica, the Dominican Republic, Haiti, Honduras, and Nicaragua, where a multiyear campaign

---

[102] Smedley Butler, "War is a Racket," *Common Sense*, vol. 4, no. 11 (November, 1935), 8.

[103] John Furlong, *Military Notes on Cuba* (Government Printing Office, 1909); Allan Millett, *Politics of Intervention: The Military Occupation of Cuba, 1906-1909* (Ohio State University Press, 1968), 122–123; Louis Perez, *Army Politics in Cuba, 1898-1956* (University of Pittsburgh Press, 1976).

[104] Leland Johnson, "U.S. Business Interests in Cuba and the Rise of Castro," *World Politics*, vol. 17, no. 3 (April 1965), 440–459, esp. 442–443.

attacked nationalist Augusto Cesar Sandino in favor of more pliant politicians.[105]

The United States intervened in Mexican politics nine times during the two decades that bracketed the First World War. In 1914, President Woodrow Wilson dispatched the Marines to take the port city of Vera Cruz as what he called a "fulcrum" from which to apply pressure to the Mexican government under General Victoriano Huerta. Once the Marines secured an entry point in the heart of Mexico, General Frederick Funston arrived with a brigade of army soldiers and set about to reestablish local governance. He banned gambling, drug sales, bull fighting, and cockfighting, and he ordered soldiers to improve schools, hospitals, and roads around Vera Cruz. By November, Huerta's government had fallen, replaced by a more liberal one under Venustiano Carranza.[106] Though this regime change had been Wilson's aim for the limited intervention, the United States continued to withhold recognition of the new Mexican government until it demonstrated democratic reforms. Carranza, rather than follow this new demand, began a proxy war on his northern border, as he encouraged regular officers to work with groups of bandits on cross-border raids.

The Mexican government backed off from official support to *banditos* over the following year, but raiding had become too profitable for some outlaws to resist. Pancho Villa, an enemy of the Carranza regime, rose to prominence during this period. In March 1916, the United States sent General John Pershing with a mere 12,000 troops into the growing civil war between Carranza and Villa, whose combined forces totaled 180,000. Pershing, whose previous assignment consisted of fighting with a free hand in the Philippines against the Moros, fumed at the limited mandate for his new command. The Wilson government held him back to only the northern and western borders of Chihuahua state. Like Funston's earlier Vera Cruz campaign, Pershing's goal was not to occupy Mexican territory, but to put pressure on Mexican politicians. The operations failed to arrest Villa himself, but the U.S. army dismantled his network as they killed most of his top generals. Innovative uses of armored motor cars and airplanes for reconnaissance enabled successful raids on fortified *haciendas*.[107] Yet military leaders recorded few lessons on fighting criminal

---

[105] Andrew Bacevich, *Diplomat in Khaki: Major General Frank Ross McCoy and American Foreign Policy, 1898-1949* (University of Kansas Press, 1989), 114–137.

[106] Birtle, vol. 1, 192–197; Robert Quirk, *An Affair of Honor: Woodrow Wilson and the Occupation of Veracruz* (University of Kentucky Press, 1962); Jack Sweetman, *Landing at Veracruz* (Naval Institute Press, 1968).

[107] Birtle, vol. 1, 202–208; James Shannon, "With the Apache Scouts in Mexico," *Cavalry Journal*, vol. 27 (January 1917), 539–557; Clarence Clendenen, *Blood on the Border: The U.S. Army and the Mexican Irregulars* (Macmillan, 1969).

insurgents in doctrine, given global preoccupation with the major war then raging between the European powers.

## 4.2 Asymmetry and the First World War

First World War studies have tended to focus on conventional operations of the Western Front, whereas asymmetry was typical in other theaters of the war. In the naval competition between the powerful British navy and their German upstart rivals, the latter began "unrestricted" use of submarines and torpedoes, much cheaper to produce than the battleships seen at the time as the standards of naval power. But the British provoked asymmetric warfare, as well. T.E. Lawrence, depicted in Figure 5, aided the rebellion of Arab tribes led by Emir Faisal against their former patrons in the Ottoman Empire. Lawrence detailed his experiences in *The Seven Pillars of Wisdom* (1926), a rich literary elaboration on his "27 Articles," a didactic text issued to British colonial troops in 1917. Throughout both works, Lawrence counseled imperial patrons of insurgents to adopt an empathetic, even indulgent, mien. He wrote in the Articles, "Do not try to do too much with your own hands. Better the Arabs do it tolerably than you do it perfectly. It is their war, and you are to help them, not to win it for them."[108] It was an early recognition of the limits of the stronger power as patron to asymmetric warfare.

Above all, Lawrence noted the shift in temporal mindset necessary for colonial operations. Whereas conventional military commanders strove for

**Figure 5** T.E. Lawrence, photograph by Lowell Thomas, 1919, Wikimedia Commons

---

[108] Thomas Edward Lawrence, *27 Articles* (New York: Simon and Schuster, 2017), 2.

strict obedience and lightning-quick campaigns, Lawrence argued that "war upon rebellion" was "messy and slow, like eating soup with a knife."[109] As recent events have demonstrated in the former British Palestine, slow operations may take on multigenerational proportions. Egypt's Muslim brotherhood, as well as Zionist militias such as Lehi, waged violence during the interwar period against British imperial police forces. The interminable terror campaigns provided motivation for the British to depart from the region after the Second World War.[110]

British armies in Africa during the First World War fought another counterguerrilla campaign. German General Paul Lettow von Vorbeck, who had previously supervised a genocidal repression of the Herero people, led a few thousand Germans and more than ten thousand indigenous *askari* forces on a herculean march across the German colony, as they avoided larger British formations and sabotaged their lines of communication.[111] Lettow von Vorbeck was the only German officer to invade British imperial territory during the war. He was so successful in his evasion of the British that his forces ignored the armistice date of November 11 and did not surrender until two weeks later, once they realized their government had capitulated. Historical memory of this campaign has tended toward hagiography, with focus on the German commander's cultivation of "loyal" African auxiliaries. More recent works have turned critical attention to the fundamental exploitation that colonialism entailed. Since he was surrounded by enemy colonizers from the start of the war, Lettow von Vorbeck could not hope for a true victory. Instead, he used the people and resources of the German colony in a cruel calculus, as means to the end of waylaying British imperial troops that London sought to transfer out of Africa to the Western Front.[112]

Across the French Empire, the Great War produced conditions that encouraged rebellion. Not only did the fighting in Europe increase demands for colonial resources, in particular for labor and military service, but there were fewer French troops available to police the colonies. These trends reinforced nascent nationalist sentiment in Indochina, Algeria, and Niger, where major

---

[109] Thomas Edward Lawrence, *Seven Pillars of Wisdom* (London, 1926), Chapter XXXIII; John Nagl, *Learning to Eat Soup with a Knife: Counterinsurgency Lessons from Malaya and Vietnam* (University of Chicago, 2005).

[110] Laleh Khalili, "The Location of Palestine in Global Counterinsurgencies," *International Journal of Middle East Studies*, vol. 42, no. 3 (July 2010), 413–433; Tom Segev, *One Palestine, Complete: Jews and Arabs Under the British Mandate* (Picador, 2001), 415–443, 472–486.

[111] Hull, *Absolute Destruction*, 37–40, 147–148.

[112] Michelle Moyd, *Violent Intermediaries: African Soldiers, Conquest, and Everyday Colonialism in German East Africa* (Ohio University Press, 2014), 7–8; John Iliffe, *A Modern History of Tanganyika* (Cambridge University Press, 1979), 241.

revolts took place in 1916. French authorities responded in a harsh manner due to the wartime legal regime, and the events only increased the extant prewar rationale for development of intelligence services abroad. The very concept of "peacetime" could be problematic in the colonies, where French observers found active surveillance necessary to forestall the ever-present threat of unrest.[113]

## 4.3 The "Interwar" Period in Ireland and Ethiopia

The period between the world wars contained many examples of anti-imperial combat. Two notable examples included the Irish Republican movement against the occupying British and Ethiopian resistance against an Italian invasion. These conflicts attracted special attention in the United States, the former because of its Irish-American population, and the latter due to the importance of an independent black empire to African-American culture.

In Ireland, the rebels' ability to recruit international support comprised a key prerequisite. Historian J. Joseph Lee summarized the importance of the United States to Irish independence by concluding, "No America, no New York, no Easter Rising." Five of the seven signatories to the 1916 proclamation of rebellion had lived in the United States, and the document claimed that Ireland's rebels were "supported by her exiled children in America."[114] While there is no doubt funds crossed the Atlantic from that point until the Free State emerged in 1922, U.S. support paled compared to contributions from Germany in the early years of the rebellion.

American public sentiment turned in favor of Irish independence after intense British reprisals, which a leading literary figure in the United States called "too much like the shooting of prisoners of war," and which hurt Britain's purported status as a defender of small nations.[115] By the end of the First World War, the separatist political party Sinn Fein gained the majority of seats in Irish elections, and by 1919 Irish politicians declared a revolutionary assembly. Sinn Fein often exaggerated the amount of diaspora support it received from Irish-Americans. The U.S. government maintained its official sympathies with the U.K. throughout

---

[113] Jonathan Krause, "Rebellion and Resistance in French Indochina in the First World War," *Journal of Imperial and Commonwealth History*, vol. 48, no. 3, pp. 425–455; Krause, "Islam and Anti-Colonial Rebellions in North and West Africa, 1914-1918," *The Historical Journal*, vol. 64, no. 3 (June 2021), 674–695; Martin Thomas, *Empires of Intelligence: Security Services and Colonial Disorder After 1914* (University of California Press, 2008), esp. Chapters 3 and 5.

[114] Lee cited in Miriam Grey, *Ireland's Allies: America and the 1916 Easter Rising* (University College Dublin Press, 2016), 1.

[115] Francis Carroll, *America and the Making of an Independent Ireland: A History* (New York University Press, 2021).

the Great War and afterward, even as diplomats encouraged their ally to be lenient toward rebel prisoners.[116]

British governments since the late 19th century had contemplated Home Rule for Ireland, a policy that proposed to keep the island under British Dominion as a single political unit responsible for its own internal government. The British strategy in 1919 was to use an overwhelming force of occupation to stabilize the Ireland long enough to accept a treaty of Dominion status, which occurred in 1921. The offer caused a split in the independence movement, as Northern Ireland formed its own Parliament in alliance with the United Kingdom. Some Irish revolutionaries accepted leadership of the southern Catholic Free State, but a hard core of IRA leaders fought an unsuccessful civil war against the new Irish government until 1923. The chain of events demonstrated that spectacular episodes of violence did little to alter public perceptions of political legitimacy. The vast majority of the Irish populace supported the IRA in 1921 against the British, but not the following year in its struggle against the new state based in Dublin.[117]

The Irish War for Independence (1920–1921) pitted the Republican Army (IRA) and various other militias against a British military augmented by the Black and Tan police force and by Belfast-based Protestant militias. British forces were more numerous and better equipped than the Catholic rebels, who benefited instead from a near-monopoly on intelligence. The imbalances made the fighting incoherent and prone to blind ambushes, double-dealing, and executions of alleged spies. Much of the historiography of the revolution focused on atrocities committed by British forces, but more recent accounts have been more balanced in their exposition of IRA abuses. Due to the degeneration of the conflict into popular religious violence, especially in the cities of Dublin and Belfast, one historian assessed, "by 1921, both the IRA and Crown forces were shooting civilians more than they shot each other."[118] Recent historians, despite the heroic narratives that laud IRA leaders such as Michael Collins, have acknowledged that actual fighting was limited compared to other 20th-century wars of national liberation. The IRA's successes took place more in the realms of "intelligence and publicity" than in street fighting.[119]

---

[116] Bernadette Whelan, *United States Foreign Policy and Ireland: From Empire to Independence, 1913-29* (Four Courts Press, 2006).

[117] Bill Kissane, "From the Outside In: the International Dimension to the Irish Civil War," in John Gibney, ed., *The Irish War of Independence and Civil War* (Pen and Sword, 2020), 121–126; Peter Hart, *The IRA at War, 1916-1923* (Oxford University Press, 2003), 25.

[118] Hart, *IRA at War*, 19.

[119] Michael Hopkinson, *The Irish War of Independence* (McGill University Press, 2002), xviii; for a comprehensive account of the Irish war for independence, see Charles Townshend, *The Republic: The Fight for Irish Independence* (Allen Lane, 2013).

Whereas Ireland's conflict took place in the context of decolonization, the Second Italo-Ethiopian War (1935–1937) was an unabashed European land grab against an independent African empire. The latter war revealed the fascist tendency toward militarized rule at the same time that British and French governments began to entertain peaceful transitions out of empire for some colonized peoples. Despite widespread condemnation of the situation developing in Ethiopia, the U.S. government remained neutral, which in effect benefited the Italians. Though more than 10,000 African-American men petitioned to enlist in the conflict, neutrality law prevented volunteers from traveling to either belligerent country. Italian-Americans tended to support the Mussolini government in the mid-1930s, but there was little desire among European emigrants and their descendants to return to the homeland, only to fight in Africa. There were material interests at hand, as well, in terms of U.S. commodities trade. The wartime breaking of the Italian-American treaty of commerce allowed for important exceptions, including for food and petroleum products. American oil companies tripled shipments to Italy during the first months of the invasion.[120]

One remarkable example of American assistance to the Ethiopian Empire emerged with the August 1935 appointment of Tuskegee Airman Col. John C. Robinson as the head of Selassie's fledgling air forces. Yet Robinson soon became disillusioned, as his idealized Pan-Africanism conflicted with the practice of slavery in Ethiopia. Slavery was a millennium-old tradition in the region, rooted in endemic conflict between rival Muslim and Christian polities. The war against Italy exposed the issue on the global stage. Mussolini claimed to be waging a "civilizing" campaign to abolish slavery, whereas Selassie had to expand slave raids in order to entice regional strongmen to support him in battle.[121]

The fighting included some of the most lopsided skirmishes in recent memory, and both sides resorted to atrocities. Ethiopian troops used "dumdum" bullets outlawed by the 1925 Geneva Convention, and some units executed captured Italian and Eritrean laborers. Italian excesses came mostly from above. Whereas the Ethiopian Air Force led by Robinson consisted of fewer than twenty airplanes, none armed with weapons, the Italians boasted more than 450 aircraft, including the new S.81 heavy bomber shown in Figure 6. The Italians used air forces to overcome an inferiority in ground troops and the harsh terrain of Ethiopia's interior highlands. British observer General J.F.C. Fuller commented that the Italian use of sulfur

---

[120] Zara Steiner, *The Triumph of the Dark: European International History, 1933-1939* (Oxford University Press, 2011), 110.

[121] Phillip Thomas Tucker, *Father of the Tuskegee Airmen, John C. Robinson* (Potomac Books, 2012), 155–158.

**Figure 6** S.81 airplane, c. 1940, Wikimedia Commons

mustard gas to deny mountain passes and immobilize retreating Ethiopian units was an "exceedingly cunning use of this chemical," whereas Emperor Selassie complained that the gas attacks were imprecise, harmful to soldiers and civilians alike. Foreign observers estimated that the outlawed chemical agents caused about one third of the Ethiopians' 50,000 casualties throughout the war.[122]

The League of Nations offered only half-hearted sanctions against Italy in response. The effects of the sanctions did less to impede Mussolini and his generals as to spur them into faster offensive action, to complete their conquest before disruptions to the Italian economy became burdensome. The Suez Canal remained open to Italian vessels carrying war materiel to the front, and all penalties ended when the Italians sacked the Ethiopian capital of Addis Abba in May 1936. The disappointing results of the war for the Pan-African movement resulted in its political radicalization. The Euro-Americans' apathy toward the sovereignty of a black nation suggested they could not be relied upon in the future. Segregated units of African-Americans and colonial troops had served in great numbers in the First World War; by the time of the Second, they became

---

[122] John Frederick Charles Fuller, "The Italo-Ethiopian War: a Military Analysis by an Eye-witness Observer," *Army Ordnance*, vol. XVI, no. 96, 340–348, esp. 347; Giorgio Rochat, "The Italian Air Force in the Ethiopian War, 1935-1936," in Ruth Ben-Ghiat and Mia Fuller, eds., *Italian Colonialism* (Springer, 2016), 37–57, esp. 38–40; Lina Grip and John Hart, "The use of chemical weapons in the 1935-36 Italo-Ethiopian War," SIPRI Arms Control and Non-proliferation Program, October 2009, 3–4.

more invested in causes such as the "double V" campaign in the United States: victory not only over the Axis powers, but against racism at home.[123]

The Italians' gains in Ethiopia proved harmful to the stability of their empire in the long term. Although Mussolini proclaimed victory upon his troops' occupation of the Ethiopian capital city, warlords in the country's interior led a popular resistance that became widespread through the end of 1937 and escalated after 1939, as the British and French governments began to aid the insurgents. The Italians never exercised effective control over their claimed colony, which instead strained its military resources. When the Allies liberated Ethiopia during the Second World War, Haile Selassie returned to leadership and John Robinson joined him to found the country's first commercial airline.

## 4.4 The Second World War

During the First World War, individual British and German officers sponsored national separatist movements against rival empires. A generation later, partisan fighting was more organic and widespread. The harsh military rule that the Axis powers exported resulted in consistent attempts at resistance. Opposition to Imperial Japan and Nazi Germany bred "free" partisan units that fought alongside Allied formations, covert organizations engaged in sabotage, and ad hoc instances of disruption to occupation governments by more or less ordinary civilians.[124] Opinions differed, however, about the military effectiveness of popular resistance. General officers on both sides of the conflict estimated that civilians in France shortened the war in Western Europe by six months, whereas one economic historian rated this effort as the "least successful" and "most costly" investment the Allies made in that theater.[125]

American officers, tasked to support wartime governance in Europe and Asia in the wakes of Axis retreats, divided in their opinions about the ethos of military occupation. Whereas army doctrine, FM 27-5, counseled "just, considerate, and mild treatment" in order to "convert enemies into friends," a top instructor at the School of Military Government disagreed with this lenient approach. "There is only one legitimate objective of military government, and

---

[123] Joseph Harris, *African-American Reactions to War in Ethiopia, 1936-1941* (Louisiana State University Press, 1994).

[124] Colin Heaton, *German Anti-Partisan Warfare in Europe, 1939-1945* (Schiffer, 2001); Olivier Wieviorka, *The French Resistance* (Harvard University Press, 2016); Jadwiga Bipukspa, *Survivors: Warsaw under Nazi Occupation* (Cambridge University Press, 2022); James Villanueva, *Awaiting MacArthur's Return: World War II Guerrilla Resistance Against the Japanese in the Philippines* (Kansas University Press, 2022).

[125] For civilian resistance as effective, see Michael Richard Daniell Foot, *S.O.E. in France: An Account of the Work of the British Special Operations Executive in France, 1940-1944* (Crown, 1966), ix; for a rebuttal, see Alan Milward, "Effectiveness of Resistance," in *Resistance in Europe, 1939-1945*, eds. Stephen Hawes and Ralph White (Allen Lane, 1975), 202.

that is to win the war," he concluded. "It is a method of fighting behind the lines, and is done by holding the civil population in subjection."[126] The new edition of the manual published in 1943 seemed to reflect this hardening of philosophy, as it scrapped "considerate and mild treatment" of civilians and substituted "reasonable treatment" instead.[127] In the balance between firmness and fairness, most military officers tended toward the former.

Another significant aspect of asymmetry to emerge from the Second World War resulted from closer cooperation between government officials and scientists to develop new methods of destruction. In Germany, Adolf Hitler hoped in vain that his experimental V2 rocket program could turn the tide against the more numerous military forces of his enemies. The United States countered by spending over \$2 billion on the Manhattan Project to develop nuclear weapons.[128] In the aftermath of the atomic bombs dropped on Hiroshima and Nagasaki in August 1945, military thinkers speculated about a future of warfare measured by airborne ordnance rather than men, guns, and vehicles. Some historians argued that the Americans had used the bombs more as a means of menacing their emergent Cold War foes in the U.S.S.R. than to finish the war against a subdued Japanese military, which by that point lacked effective naval and air forces.[129]

## 4.5 Postwar Conflicts: China, Greece, and the Philippines

Despite speculation about the potential of nuclear weapons to render conventional wars obsolete, limited conflicts on land and sea continued to occur. A new bipolarity of communist and capitalist states emerged, led by the U.S.S.R. and the United States, respectively. Asymmetric conflicts proliferated along the borders between the spheres of influence. Civil wars emerged in China, Greece, and the Philippines, among other places, which pitted left and right wings of war-era resistance movements against each other.

The most significant fighting in geopolitical terms took place in China, where communist forces under Mao Tse Tung had opposed nationalist forces under Chiang Kai-shek since 1927. Combat between the two sides subsided as they

---

[126] Andrew J. Birtle, *U.S. Counterinsurgency and Contingency Operations Doctrine, 1942-1976*, vol. 2 (Washington, DC: Center of Military History, 2006), 12.

[127] FM 27-5, *Military Government* (1940), p. 4; FM 27-5, *U.S. Army and Navy Manual of Military Government and Civil Affairs* (1943), 7–8.

[128] Kevin O'Neill, "Building the Bomb," in *Atomic Audit: The Costs and Consequences of U.S. Nuclear Weapons since 1940*, ed. Stephen Schwartz (Brookings, 2011), 63.

[129] Gar Alperovitz, *Atomic Diplomacy* (Simon and Schuster, 1965); Tsuyoshi Hasegawa, *Racing the Enemy: Stalin, Truman, and the Surrender of Japan* (Harvard University Press, 2005); J. Samuel Walker, *Prompt and Utter Destruction: Truman and the Use of Atomic Bombs Against Japan* (University of North Carolina Press, 2016).

both opposed the Japanese invasion during the Second World War, but resumed when foreign occupation waned. At that point, the United States began to provide aid to the nationalists. The United States lent support on a conditional basis at first, in hopes that Chiang might undertake democratic reforms in exchange for more arms shipments. As the communists gained ground, however, the Truman administration dropped their conditions and escalated support, as they sent an advisory group by late 1947. Americans offered a holistic approach to warfare that aimed for competence in both conventional and irregular fighting. General David Barr advised the Chinese to form light divisions, as opposed to the U.S. affinity for firepower, in consideration of the relative lack of artillery and tanks that Chiang could acquire. In keeping with the American tradition, however, Barr urged Chiang to consolidate his dispersed formations and adopt an aggressive, offensive ethos.[130]

Scholars have downplayed the tactical and technical aspects of the Chinese Civil War compared to more fundamental relationships between Chiang, Mao, and the peasant population. The reputation of Chiang's Kuomintang (KMT) suffered from its failure to halt the Japanese occupation of China during the Second World War; the Japanese-installed puppet government framed itself as anti-communist, which encouraged the rural peasantry to identify more with leftist resistance.[131]

Mao, depicted in Figure 7, codified guidance to his troops in the popular *Little Red Book*. He advised his army to move through the people like a "fish in water," and thereby forged a politico-military structure that proved immune to territorial gains by the nationalists. Mao proposed a three-stage model of asymmetric warfare. First, a withdrawal of military forces was necessary to build political cadres. Phase 2 consisted of guerrilla campaigns alongside the establishment of military bases in liberated areas. Finally, a conventional strategic offensive could ensue. Communist soldiers received orders to abide by an "eight-point covenant," which emphasized positive relations with civilians: "speak politely, pay fairly for what you buy, return everything you borrow, pay for anything you damage, do not hit or swear at people, do not damage crops, do not take liberties with women, and do not ill-treat captives." For his part, Chiang too recognized the political and economic nature of the struggle. His government's "Manual for Bandit Suppression" (1933, 1945) concluded, "the sure road to the extinction of the Reds must take as its point of departure the abstention from annoying the people." But nationalist troops in the field demonstrated this was easier said than done. Mao's forces, buoyed by the tide of

---

[130] William H. Mott IV, *Military Assistance: An Operational Perspective* (Bloomsbury, 1999), 135–137.

[131] Chalmers Johnson, *Peasant Nationalism and Communist Power in China* (University of California, 1962).

**Figure 7** Mao Tse Tung addresses followers, December 6, 1944, Franklin
D. Roosevelt Library, Public Domain Photographs, NARA, Wikimedia
Commons

popular sentiment developed over the course of decades, swept their rivals off
the mainland by 1949.[132]

In Greece, after the Axis powers withdrew from the peninsula at the end of
the Second World War, British agents helped the monarchists to restore a right-
leaning government. The new Greek state began to persecute political opposition, which rebranded as the Democratic People's Army, modeled on Mao's
example. About 30,000 guerrilla fighters operated in small groups, ambushed
soft targets, and withdrew to safe havens with communist neighbors to the north
in Albania, Bulgaria, and Yugoslavia. The rebels found broad popular support in
the *yiafka*, secret cells of civilians who provided intelligence, labor, supplies,
and money. British and American advisors to the Greek government combined
conventional operations with public works projects for the rural poor. But
government forces employed harsh measures against civilians, as well. They
executed tens of thousands and relocated hundreds of thousands more, in an

---

[132] Birtle, vol. 2, 36–40; "Manual for Bandit Suppression," (Chinese Government Press, 1945), 7;
Mao Tse Tung, "Proclamation of the Chinese People's Liberation Army," April 25, 1949.

attempt to drain the water and leave the insurgency's fish flopping on deserted land. It is difficult to assess which, if any, of these methods was effective, since the end of the fighting had more to do with unfortunate developments for the rebel side. Greek communist leader Nikos Zachariades made an ill-conceived move to the strategic offensive before he had built necessary support among the people. To compound the error, political disagreements with Yugoslavia's Tito closed off safe havens for Greek rebels in the north. By the end of 1949, the U.S.-backed government held firm control over the country.[133]

In the Philippines, the withdrawal of the Japanese at the end of the Second World War ignited a bloody internal contest between right-wing forces, many of which had been Axis collaborators, and a left-leaning resistance army, the Huk Balahap. Heavy-handed political tactics by the new Filipino government led to a surge of support for the Huks, who were led by General Luis Taruc, and bolstered by village logistical support of the Barrio United Defense Corps of central Luzon. The United States deployed a military assistance group to advise the government in their counterinsurgency efforts. Among the most consequential reforms was the elimination of habeas corpus for suspected rebels. Though contrary to American political theory, the reform was framed as a humanitarian measure, since extant laws that demanded the rapid release of prisoners often tempted government forces to execute captives in transit.

The defeat of the Huk rebellion came under the direction of Ramon Magsaysay, the Philippines defense secretary and former Second World War guerrilla fighter, who waged his campaign with a "left hand of friendship" and a "right hand of force." Magsaysay sent top officers to study in the United States, adopted training manuals from the American assistance group, and created an elite Scout Ranger force to pursue Taruc's insurgent army, whose ranks had swelled to over 15,000 men by 1950. In terms of friendship toward the rural people, the government built schools, dug wells, and distributed food and medical supplies to remote locales. One noteworthy campaign was the Economic Development Corps (EDC), which built farms in the jungle, led by Magsaysay's cadres and worked by captured Huk fighters. The program undercut the Huk slogan of "land for the landless," and thus served as a major propaganda coup for the government. Still, the program was more rhetoric than reality; by 1959, fewer than 6,000 people had been resettled on EDC farms, while the ratio of landless farmers in the country soared to 70 percent

---

[133] Birtle, vol. 2, 44–54; Howard Jones, *"A New Kind of War": America's Global Strategy and the Truman Doctrine in Greece* (Oxford University Press, 1989); Andre Gerolymatos, *An International Civil War: Greece, 1943-1949* (Yale University Press, 2016); Spyridon Plakoudas, *The Greek Civil War: Strategy, Counterinsurgency, and the Monarchy* (I.B. Taurus, 2017)

by 1963. In the meantime, the state's aggressive campaigns against Taruc scattered his forces and resulted in his 1954 surrender.[134]

The military partnership between the Philippines and the United States continued after the Huk threat dissipated, as the leasing of naval bases, combined training operations, and intelligence sharing have continued to the present day. The continuity in U.S. support to the Philippines demonstrates the importance of counterinsurgency as a means of modern development in the American-led economic system. The unbroken flow of armed conflict after the end of the Second World War, not only in the Philippines, Greece, and China, but also in Malaya, Indonesia, and elsewhere, demonstrated the porous boundary between wartime and peacetime, as resistance movements established by the Allies to defeat the Axis used their weapons and training for unforeseen purposes in the absence of the overarching wartime alliance structure.

## 5 Asymmetry and Cold War (1950–1990)

After the Second World War, two trends began to tilt the balance further in favor of insurgencies: international law and a bipolar world order. The Geneva Conventions of 1949, due to signatories' support for antifascist militias during the last war, granted official recognition to internal resistance movements. This was a controversial measure due to its potential to limit state sovereignty, an urgent concern amid ongoing race riots and anti-colonial rebellions, so the finalized legal text contained vague language and potential loopholes. The conventions furthermore made collective punishment and reprisals against civilians illegal, whereas these practices had been common elements of counterinsurgency before. But noncombatants comprised another grey area: Could people be defined as such if they aided rebels with logistics, shelter, or intelligence? Despite a lack of definitive answers, the spirit of the convention indicated a shift in legal norms toward restraint of powerful state militaries.[135]

Along with growing demands for humanitarianism, a Cold War commenced between the emergent superpowers of the United States and the Soviet Union, which supplied military assistance to respective allies around the world. U.S. President Harry Truman, in response to Soviet repression in Eastern Europe and the militarization of the Berlin boundary, promised to aid "free peoples who are resisting subjugation by armed minorities or outside pressures."

---

[134] Birtle, vol. 2, 56–65; see also Lawrence Greenberg, *The Hukbalahap Insurrection: A Case Study of a Successful Anti-Insurgency Operation in the Philippines, 1946-1955* (RAND, 1987); Jacqueline Hazelton, *Bullets Not Ballots: Success in Counterinsurgency Warfare* (Cornell University Press, 2021), 48–80.

[135] Boyd van Dijk, *Preparing for War: The Making of the 1949 Geneva Conventions* (Oxford University Press, 2022).

Truman introduced a holistic program that sent economic assistance to European states through the Marshall Plan along with the deployment of military advisors. The United States created the North Atlantic Treaty Organization (NATO) in 1949 and the Southeast Asian Treaty Organization (SEATO) in 1954, institutions which spread tens of billions of dollars to strengthen the militaries of more than forty countries throughout the 1950s.[136] The Soviet Union, by contrast, could not afford such comprehensive aid programs due to the ruinous effects of the German invasion on its economy. Furthermore, early Marxist thinkers had scant optimism for rural guerrilla warfare. Soviet leadership considered urban coups d'état and conventional war to be more significant military means. It was only with Mao's stunning victory in China that military officers in the U.S.S.R. began to recognize the potential of arming peasant movements. In 1961, Premier Nikita Khrushchev escalated foreign aid with a pledge to support "national liberation" fronts around the world.[137] Asymmetric wars abounded in the context of superpower proxy conflicts, notably in Korea, Vietnam, and Afghanistan.

## 5.1 The Korean War (1950–1953)

The Korean Peninsula had been a Japanese colony since 1910. Japan's withdrawal in 1945 led the United Nations to divide the territory into a Northern state organized by former guerrilla Kim Il Sung and a Southern state under Christian missionary Syngman Rhee. Popular opposition to the brutal and corrupt Rhee regime began even before the outbreak of war in June 1950, as North Korean agents infiltrated the territory of their southern neighbor. Communist sentiment was especially strong on the southern island of Jeju. The forces arrayed against the brewing insurgency comprised regular Republic of Korea (ROK) soldiers, national police, and the private armies of anti-communist politicians that Rhee co-opted. An initial period of forced migration, mass arrests, and executions gave way by 1949 to a policy of "half force, half administration." By then, more than 40,000 homes had been destroyed and 100,000 people in Jeju relocated. The U.S. army assisted Rhee in creating a "central intelligence agency" to coordinate information drawn from the many stripes of armed forces, and the improved picture of the population allowed Rhee to offer amnesty to former communist enemies through the National Repentance Alliance. Armed propaganda teams called "Listen to

---

[136] Benn Steil, *The Marshall Plan: The Dawn of the Cold War* (Simon and Schuster, 2018), 175, 227; Ang Cheng Guan, *The Southeast Asia Treaty Organization* (Routledge, 2022).

[137] Birtle, vol. 2, 23–25.

Me" units paired government officials with schoolchildren, who visited remote villages bearing pamphlets and films.[138]

Kim Il Sung, after he failed to subvert the South by infiltration, turned to a conventional invasion in the summer of 1950. The rapid advance and still more rapid retreat of the communist forces trapped large groups of North Korean soldiers and sympathetic civilians behind the lines of the conventional war. As a result, about a third of all UN forces by the end of 1950 had to be designated for rear-area security operations (a similar proportion to that of Union troops at the height of the U.S. Civil War). In addition to the tried and true methods of encirclement and isolation against pockets of resistance, the United States experimented with new units and technologies. The Marine Corps used helicopters for the first time as spotters for their patrols. Eighth Army headquarters in 1950 created the first Ranger companies, led by former Philippine Scout Colonel John McGee. U.S. planes dropped more than twelve million propaganda leaflets on enemy fighters and civilians. An example of the leaflet deployment system is shown in Figure 8. Though the leaflets led to just three hundred enemy surrenders, the tactic indicated growing attention in the United States to the promise of psychological warfare.[139]

As in the Philippines, the carrot-and-stick approach to counterguerrilla operations continued in Korea. The UN Civil Assistance Command fed and clothed more than four million refugees, vaccinated sixty million, and worked to improve water and sanitation infrastructure in efforts to win over local populations. However, military commanders continued to lean on the stick of U.S. firepower, as they devastated the Korean countryside to force partisan fighters out of rural shelters, especially during the bitter winter months. By the spring of 1951, as the conflict devolved into stalemate, the combination of North Korean military retreat, surrenders, and casualties had reduced the number of insurgents in South Korea by half.[140]

Experience in Korea pushed U.S. military leadership to develop doctrine for fighting guerrillas. Lieutenant Colonel Russell Volckmann, who had operated in the Japanese-occupied Philippines during the Second World War, led publication efforts. Volckmann augmented his own beliefs about insurgencies with the 1944 German manual "Fighting the Guerrilla Bands," as well as U.S. army-commissioned pamphlets written by German veterans. American interest in

---

[138] Birtle, vol. 2, 89–97; Soul Park, "The Unnecessary Uprising: Jeju Island rebellion and South Korean Counterinsurgency Experience, 1947-1948," *Small Wars and Insurgencies*, vol. 21, no. 2 (June 2010), 359–381.

[139] "Psychological Warfare in Korea: an Interim Report," *Public Opinion Quarterly*, vol. 15, no. 1 (Spring 1951), pp. 65–75; Herbert Avedon, "War for Men's Minds," *Military Review*, vol. 33 (March 1954), 53–60.

[140] Birtle, vol. 2, 98–115.

**Figure 8** Korean War leaflet bomb, U.S. Army photograph, 1950, Wikimedia Commons

*Wehrmacht* counterinsurgency campaigns resonated with more general efforts to learn lessons about fighting communist forces in Eastern Europe. U.S. officials proved ambivalent about the Nazi performance in occupied territories, as they noted that brutal treatment of civilians often bred insurgency while at the same time commending the operational skill of the *Wehrmacht*. German-inspired theory remained consistent with what the United States had practiced throughout its own history: (1) to isolate fighters from the population, by forced migration if necessary, (2) to deny guerrillas foreign aid, and (3) to destroy the enemy through aggressive, offensive-minded patrols. These goals called for large numbers of infantry, supported by elite small units (in Germany, the *Jagdkommando*), as well as by local civilians to be recruited as guides, spies, and auxiliaries. Volckmann's FM 31-20, *Special Operations Techniques*, was published in February 1951, though draft manuals had been rushed to Korea to assist commanders in clearing their rear areas of enemy infiltrators.[141]

## 5.2 Wars of Decolonization

Historians have held up the British campaign in Malaya (1948–1960) as an exemplary episode of counterinsurgency operations. Unlike contemporary efforts by the French and the Americans, the British succeeded in defeating a communist guerrilla threat to governance. British forces followed three guiding principles: flexible military tactics, close cooperation between the military and the civil authorities, and the mass detention of suspected rebels without trial.[142] The insurgency, led by Chin Peng and his Malaysian Communist Party (MCP), probably never numbered more than 8,000 fighters, but they were backed by a much larger Min Yuen (mass organization) that provided intelligence and supplies. Chin sought to follow Mao's three-phase guidance on warfare, but his attempt to transition to phase two in 1949, with the building of bases in "liberated areas" protected by large units, proved to be premature. As a result, Chin shifted strategy in October 1951 to focus on political organization through propaganda and covert activities. Military forces dispersed, "waiting it out" in the deep jungle rather than contesting colonial population control at the jungle fringes.[143]

General Gerald Templer has benefited from sustained public efforts to praise his leadership of British and colonial forces. But the most credible recent account argues that Templer served merely to "optimize" a system that his predecessor, General Harold Briggs, had established by 1950. Under the Briggs Plan, British strategy shifted from hunting guerrilla bands to broader population control, which included the forced migration of over half a million people into "new villages." This strategy slowed logistical support from rural peasants to the insurgents to an ineffective trickle.

Some historians have attributed the success of the British to national charac-teristics, such as patience to test eccentric policies or the purported gentleman-liness of its officer corps. But the insurgency suffered from critical obstacles that may better explain its ineffectiveness. The movement was over 90 percent ethnic Chinese, rather than Malay, so their members were often identifiable

---

[141] Birtle, vol. 2, 134–135, 142; Robert Hutchinson, "The Weight of History: *Wehrmacht* Officers, the U.S. Army Historical Division, and U.S. Military Doctrine, 1945-1956, *Journal of Military History*, vol. 78, no. 4 (October 2014), 1321–1348.

[142] Andrew Mumford, *The Counterinsurgency Myth: The British Experience of Irregular Warfare* (Routledge, 2012), 154.

[143] Karl Hack, *The Malayan Emergency: Revolution and Counterinsurgency at the End of Empire* (Cambridge University Press, 2021), 8–10, 247–250.

among the broader population. Still, much hard fighting proved necessary. One analyst estimated the cost of each insurgent killed or captured at $200,000.[144] In the end, the British developed political solutions to end the fighting. The Chinese minority gained the right to vote, and loyalties split with the introduction of a non-communist Chinese Malaysian political party. Moreover, the imperial government decided to grant independence in 1957, as officials recalculated the asymmetric costs of guerrilla fighting compared to the dubious benefits of direct colonial government.[145]

The French military after the Second World War, by contrast, attempted to regain some of its prestige by reestablishing colonial control over Indochina. Vietnamese nationalists seeking independence adopted a Maoist strategy that consisted of three phases: withdrawal to build political cadres, guerrilla attacks against occupying forces, and finally a general offensive by conventional military units. Political leader Ho Chi Minh and his military chief Vo Nguyen Giap developed their plan during the Japanese occupation, but they shifted their target with the French return in 1946.

The asymmetries of the conflict between the French and the Viet Minh resistance split along political and material lines. The French suffered from a lack of popular support but enjoyed the unique advantage of air transport, supplied more as the years passed by the United States. In an effort to exploit this capability and strike at the rear logistic zone of communist support, General Henri Navarre developed fortified bases built up and supplied by air, known as "hedgehogs." The concept worked well in the 1952 battle of Na San, in which Giap's forces retreated after heavy losses. But the Viet Minh escalated their resistance when the French tried to occupy a more ambitious hedgehog base the following year at Dien Bien Phu. Progress of the siege turned on the insurgents' logistical supply of artillery and ammunition over mountain passes that surrounded the French base. Thanks to heroic efforts by tens of thousands of local workers, bicycles reinforced with bamboo defeated the aerial supply system of the French and their American allies. Historians continue to debate why the French surrendered their position by May of 1954: Had it been a strategic mistake to offer battle in the isolated northwest part of the colony, tactical disagreements between Navarre and his subordinate commanders, or poor morale of the French colonial troops that doomed the base?

Whatever the cause of failure, the results of Dien Bien Phu were decisive in a political, not a military, sense. French forces involved in the campaign, though they suffered a horrific mortality rate of 60 percent, comprised only a small

---

[144] Galula, *Counterinsurgency Warfare*, p. 7; David French, *The British Way in Counterinsurgency, 1945-1967* (Oxford University Press, 2011), 249–250.

[145] Hack, *Malayan Emergency*, 17–18.

fraction of the total available for colonial service. But the surrender so demoralized French politicians that they began to seek a way out of the region, rather than to reinforce the region with more troops.[146]

In Algeria, political trends likewise proved more significant than military events. There was no equivalent military defeat to shock French authorities here, as there had been in Indochina. Some National Liberation Front (FLN) leaders, such as Zighoud Youssef, sought "winning over" the Algerian population by implicating them in attacks on French military targets, in order to ensure an aggressive state backlash. French forces understood the revolutionary character of their opponents and set about to dismantle their organization by police methods, to include coercive interrogation. General Jacques Massu and his paratroopers fought a hard-won urban struggle for Algiers. By 1957, the French army had driven insurgents from the capital; subsequent operations decimated the rebellion's fighters throughout the countryside. The turning point in FLN strategy, after their failure in domestic military operations, was the formation of military units in safe havens across the border in Tunisia, and to a lesser extent in Morocco, after these states became independent from France in 1956.[147]

French military victories played into the strategy of the resistance leadership, which was consistent in its quest to internationalize the struggle. The ongoing French political repression in Algeria, in particular methods of torture, brought about scandal. Repugnant conditions amplified Arab demands, either for full political integration into the French Republic or for secession from it. Not only did ordinary people in Algeria and the metropole turn against their government's brutality, but the FLN's diplomatic campaign brought additional pressure from abroad. The French Fourth Republic abdicated power following a riot of European settlers in Algeria, and General Charles de Gaulle formed a new government in 1958 that featured a more powerful executive branch. Though de Gaulle promised at first to maintain French Algeria, he soon found that negotiation with the revolutionaries was unavoidable. Granting independence to Algeria became the only way for the French government to balance its military defenses, quell internal dissent, and maintain relationships with allies.[148]

---

[146] Bernard Fall, *Hell in a Very Small Place: the Siege of Dien Bien Phu* (Lippincott, 1967); Fredrik Logevall, *Embers of War: the Fall of an Empire and the Making of America's Vietnam* (Random House, 2012), 510–546.

[147] Saphia Arezki, "The Insurgent Strategies of the ALN in Algeria," in *Oxford Handbook on Late Colonial Insurgencies and Counter-Insurgencies*, ed. Martin Thomas and Gareth Curless (Oxford University Press, 2023), 400–411; Martin Thomas, "Policing Algeria's Borders 1956-1960: Arms Supplies, Frontier Defences and the Sakiet Affair," *War and Society*, vol. 13, no. 1 (1995), 81–99.

[148] Matthew Connelly, *A Diplomatic Revolution: Algeria's Fight for Independence and the Origins of the Post-Cold War Era* (Oxford University Press, 2002), esp. 119-141; Martin Thomas, *Fight*

The wars of decolonization became a subject of fascination for the U.S. military establishment. Americans studied less to emulate the relative success of the British, and more to avoid the pitfalls of the French. The U.S. government invited French officers to teach Americans about their recent struggles. Lieutenant Colonel David Galula, employed by Harvard and the RAND corporation, noted the key characteristic of counterinsurgency warfare was asymmetry, or the "disproportion of strength between the opponents at the outset." Whereas state forces enjoyed material advantages, the insurgent tended to have "the ideological power of a cause." Galula, following this fundamental observation, estimated that conflicts against insurgents were 80 percent political and only 20 percent military, and that intelligence, rather than firepower, was the critical variable for success. He wrote that in this kind of war, "a mimeograph machine may turn out to be more useful than a machine gun, a soldier trained as a pediatrician more important than a mortar expert, cement more wanted than barbed wire, clerks more in demand than riflemen." Though these maxims opened the door to a more humanitarian way of war, Galula admitted that pacification had to begin with an aggressive first step to destroy enemy fighters.[149]

Other French veterans took a more pessimistic viewpoint. General Paul Aussaresses, for example, counseled the use of torture and assassination as tools to combat enemies that had similar disregard for humane limitations on tactics. Aussaresses, who had served in Algeria under the notorious counter-terrorist commander Roger Trinquier, taught from his personal experiences at the U.S. Special Warfare school, founded in 1961, and later as an adviser to the military dictators of Brazil.[150]

The turn in U.S. policy toward counterinsurgency warfare was part of a broader political shift. Whereas President Dwight Eisenhower had favored "massive retaliation" with nuclear weapons as a deterrent to ground incursions, his successor John F. Kennedy preached "flexible response" through the employment of small, covert units. Academics such as Walter Rostow, who believed Maoist revolutions demanded holistic military reform, emerged as key political advisors. At an international level, policymakers in Britain, France, and the United States noted the global links between communist insurgents and

---

*or Flight: Britain, France, and their Roads from Empire* (Oxford University Press, 2014), esp. 285–345.

[149] Galula, *Counterinsurgency Warfare*, 4, 66, 76; for a critique of Galula's concepts, see Greg Daddis, *Withdrawal: Reassessing America's Final Years in Vietnam* (Oxford University Press, 2017), 76–77.

[150] Paul Aussaresses, *The Battle of the Casbah: Terrorism and Counter-Terrorism in Algeria, 1955-1957* (Enigma, 2002).

sought to share lessons among themselves in the hopes of forging a coordinated, Western counterinsurgency front.[151]

## 5.3 The United States and Vietnam (1959–1975)

The policy of flexible response led the United States to deploy military advisers around the globe, especially to the unaligned "third world" countries of Latin America, the Middle East, and Asia. Nowhere was the advisor experience more laden with consequences than in Vietnam. Upon the French exit from Indochina in 1954, the United Nations divided the Vietnamese territory into Northern and Southern states, the former led by communist agitator Ho Chi Minh and the latter by Catholic civil servant Ngo Dinh Diem. The American war foundered on a basic asymmetry of popular support for these leaders. Ho, whatever his beliefs about economic systems, was a respected nationalist throughout the peninsula, whereas Diem was corrupt and uncharismatic.[152]

The United States supplied military means to prop up the South Vietnamese government (RVN), in order to compensate for a lack of internal political support. A major turn toward escalation came in August 1964 with the Gulf of Tonkin incident, in which American naval officers claimed they had taken fire from North Vietnamese patrol-torpedo boats. Despite the dubious nature of these claims, the U.S. government responded in 1965 by deploying hundreds of thousands of men in combat units, rather than the mere thousands who made up the existing advisory effort. American military officials believed they might succeed where the French failed for two basic reasons: political and material. While the French had fought to maintain empire, the Americans sought to assist a sovereign ally, though the sheer volume of resources supplied by U.S. agents invited charges of neo-imperialism. In particular, the Americans brought much more air power to the table than the French had. U.S. pilots dropped more tonnage of munitions on Southeast Asia than on both European and Pacific theaters of the Second World War combined.[153] American air power furthermore enhanced counterinsurgency patrols on the ground. The 101st infantry

---

[151] Colin S. Gray, "What RAND Hath Wrought," *Foreign Policy*, no. 4 (Autumn, 1971), 111–129; David Milne, *America's Rasputin: Walt Rostow and the Vietnam War* (Farrar, Straus and Giroux, 2008); Élie Tenenbaum, "Beyond National Styles: Toward a Connected History of Cold War Counterinsurgency," in Heuser and Shamir, eds., *Insurgencies and Counterinsurgencies: National Styles and Strategic Cultures* (Cambridge University Press, 2016), 313–331.

[152] Fredrik Logevall, *Embers of War: The Fall of an Empire and the Making of America's Vietnam* (Random House, 2012), 639–653.

[153] Mark Clodfelter, *The Limits of Air Power: The American Bombing of North Vietnam* (Free Press, 1989); Phil Haun and Colin Jackson, "Breaker of Armies: Air Power in the Easter Offensive and the Myth of Linebacker I and II in the Vietnam War," *International Security*, vol. 40, no. 3 (Winter 2015/16), 139–178.

division led the way in training and doctrine for air assaults of helicopter-borne troops, tasked with the tactic of "search and destroy."

The North Vietnamese continued the Maoist strategy they forged against the French, in which military efforts counted for only one leg of a tripod that prioritized political and diplomatic "modes of struggle." Throughout the conflict, communist agents spent much of their energy on the political project of winning southern hearts and minds to their side and the diplomatic project of exposing "contradictions" in the enemy's camp. The American War in Vietnam was thus a hybrid conflict, fought by both insurgent communist cadres (known by the pejorative sobriquet, *Viet Cong*) and conventional North Vietnamese military units. The government in the North split between "doves," moderates who favored political solutions to the conflict, and "hawks," who preferred conventional military confrontation.[154]

The top U.S. commander, General William Westmoreland, developed a comprehensive strategy in response to this dual threat that included pacification, civic programs, and partnership with South Vietnamese forces. Yet in tactical terms, subordinates tended to focus on applying American firepower to an attrition strategy that demanded rising "body counts," set to reach a "crossover point" at which the North Vietnamese could not replace losses. A prime example of this logic at the tactical level was the battle of Ia Drang (1965), in which an American battalion led by Lieutenant Colonel Hal Moore caused heavy casualties to two North Vietnamese regiments by use of artillery and airstrikes. Artillery pieces could now be emplaced by helicopter to defend ad hoc fire bases, as seen in Figure 9. Colonel David Hackworth proposed, as an alternative to large-scale search and destroy missions, to adapt military units to become more like their guerrilla foes. Though Westmoreland instituted a "recon and commando school" in 1966, and the 173rd Airborne Brigade fielded Long Range Reconnaissance Patrol (LRRP) units, most of the U.S. military continued to fight a war for territory using firepower, much as it had during the Second World War, the defining event in the careers of most senior officers who served in Vietnam.[155]

Regardless of the casualty figures, the political campaign against foreigners and their puppet government proved irresistible for the Vietnamese people. Just as Westmoreland claimed that his forces were about to reach his victorious crossover point, General Secretary Le Duan and other hawks in the North Vietnamese government convinced General Giap to embark on a General

---

[154] Pierre Asselin, *Vietnam's American War: A History* (Cambridge University Press, 2018), 118–121.

[155] Gregory Daddis, *Westmoreland's War: Reassessing American Strategy in Vietnam* (Oxford University Press, 2014); Robert Doughty, *The Evolution of US Army Tactical Doctrine, 1946-1976* (Combat Studies Institute, 1979), 39–40.

**Figure 9** CH-47 airlift of a 155 mm howitzer, Jonathan Abel Collection, USMC
Archives, 1969, Wikimedia Commons

Offensive, General Uprising (GOGU) to correspond with the Tet holiday in
1968. Though the event was a military disaster for the North, the volume of
opposition to the South's government convinced Americans that the war could
not be won at an acceptable cost. Similar dynamics reinforced this logic
during the April 1972 Easter Offensive. In both cases, observers interpreted
the high casualties incurred by the North Vietnamese as signs of strong
political commitment.[156]

The United States did attempt some nation building efforts in the South along
with its military operations. The Civil Operations and Rural Development
(CORDS) program funded a wide range of projects, to include farm aid, medical
and educational programs, propaganda, and the establishment of law and order
through local paramilitary forces. CORDS, though envisioned as a way to
institute a kinder, gentler way of war, served mostly to generate abstract metrics
of success and overoptimistic reports. Moreover, there was a tendency even in
this program to divert funds toward military means. From 1968 to 1973,
economic aid to South Vietnam dropped by $100 million, while military aid
soared by $2 billion.[157] Westmoreland's replacement after 1968, General
Creighton Abrams, was savvy enough to ditch "body count" rhetoric in favor

---

[156] Lien-Hang T. Nguyen, *Hanoi's War: An International History of the War for Peace in Vietnam*
(University of North Carolina Press, 2012), Chapter 8.

[157] Gregory Daddis, *Withdrawal: Reassessing America's Final Years in Vietnam* (Oxford
University Press, 2017), 80–102.

of "hearts and minds." But operations did not change in a significant way; emphasis continued to favor offensive operations, with only vague notions to provide security for various development projects to follow once pacification was complete. The heavy-handedness of American bombing, combined with "harassment and interdiction" artillery and the establishment of "free fire areas," led to atrocities and damage which no amount of economic aid could repair.[158]

## 5.4 The Soviet Union in Afghanistan (1979–1989)

Britain and Russia had competed over the Central Asian borderlands in a series of wars since the 19th century. In 1978, the "Great Game" entered a new era when leftist Afghan officers seized power of their government in Kabul. The following year, the Soviet Union invaded in support of communist cadres on their southern border. Just as the Soviets and Chinese had provided aid to guerrillas in Korea and Vietnam, so the British and Americans dumped money and weapons on Pakistani intelligence agents to funnel to the anti-Soviet *mujahideen* (fighters for Islam). The system of foreign financing transformed the Afghan resistance from traditional, decentralized tribal leadership into seven new Islamist political parties.

The Red Army's strength comprised large-scale mechanized warfare designed to meet another industrial force on the plains of Europe. In Afghanistan, they found instead light infantry forces scattered throughout the Hindu Kush mountains. The Moscow government limited the deployment of soldiers to around 100,000, one fifth of whom were tied down to defend more than 800 outposts. Soviet commanders, with their troops spread thin, focused on applying their advantage in firepower over the peasant insurgency.[159] The strategy became known as "rubbleization," as the Soviets mined and bombed their way across the countryside. After villages had been hit with airstrikes or surrounded by minefields, infantry troops arrived via air assault or in mechanized vehicles to conduct raids and ambushes.

But no amount of firepower, as the Americans had learned in Vietnam, could compensate for a basic lack of enthusiasm among the population for the foreign-sponsored government. By the time the Soviets withdrew in 1989, they had lost around 14,000 soldiers killed in action. But the conflict was much graver for the Afghan people. More than one million people perished, half of all villages lay in

---

[158] Thomas C. Thayer, *War Without Fronts: The American Experience in Vietnam* (Westview Press, 1985), Chapter 12; Nick Turse, *Kill Anything That Moves: The Real American War in Vietnam* (Picador, 2014).

[159] Rodric Braithwaite, *Afgantsy: The Russians in Afghanistan, 1979-89* (Oxford University Press, 2011), 139–143.

ruins, and one third of the populace became refugees.[160] Though asymmetric wars are often limited for one side and total for the other, the Soviet war in Afghanistan provided an extreme example.

The injection of foreign military spending had outsized results for local economies in both Afghanistan and Vietnam. Popular memory of the returning Soviet veteran depicted him as laden with consumer goods nabbed on the black market: blue jeans, watches, television sets, and more. The contrasting stereotype of the American veteran, homeless and drug addled, belied the "abundance" on South Vietnamese bases that were oases of consumerism, where post exchanges hawked everything from pornographic magazines to automobiles.[161] For the counterinsurgents' home societies in the United States and the U.S.S.R., Vietnam and Afghanistan both engendered cynical distrust for the government, as rosy official reports contrasted with gloomy testimonies from those on the ground.

The collapse of the Soviet Union and the end of the bipolar era brought about neither the end of history nor the end of warfare, though violence took on a new ideological framework. Instead of the moral crusade against communism, the United States shifted to wage wars for the stated purposes of countering terrorism and responding to humanitarian crises.

## 6 Asymmetry, Rogue States, and Terrorism (1990–Present)

After the Cold War concluded, U.S. policymakers and academics used threats of non-state or "failed state" actors to maintain relevance for defense funding and to argue for military reforms. Meanwhile, revisionist governments in Russia, China, and Iran have signaled that warfare of the future will be waged by asymmetric means.

### 6.1 The Persian Gulf War (1990–1991): Revolution in Military Affairs?

As the Red Army struggled through Afghanistan and the Star Wars missile defense program made the Soviets less of an existential threat, some U.S. policymakers determined to avoid the frequent asymmetric wars of the Cold War era that had potential to flare up into Vietnam-esque quagmires.

---

[160] Louis Dupree, "Afghanistan in 1983: And Still No Solution," *Asian Survey*, vol. 24, no. 2 (February 1984), 229-239, for "rubbleization," see 234; Lester Grau, ed. *The Bear Went Over the Mountain: Soviet Combat Tactics in Afghanistan* (Frank Cass, 1998); Ali Ahmad Jalali and Lester W. Grau, *The Other Side of the Mountain: Mujahideen Tactics in the Soviet-Afghan War* (Marine Corps Studies and Analysis Division, 1995).

[161] Svetlana Alexievich, *Zinky Boys: Soviet Voices from the Afghanistan War* (W.W. Norton, 1992), Preface; Meredith Lair, *Armed with Abundance: Consumerism and Soldiering in the Vietnam War* (University of North Carolina Press, 2011).

U.S. armed forces embarked on a series of campaigns throughout the 1980s in Grenada, Panama, Lebanon, Haiti, and El Salvador. Concerns about these uses of force, acute after Hezbollah agents' 1983 bombing of the U.S. embassy and Marine Corps barracks in Lebanon, manifested in the Colin Powell–Caspar Weinberger doctrine. This counsel of restraint advised certain prerequisites before the U.S. military deployed to a conflict: a clear exit strategy, an overwhelming initial deployment of force rather than incremental steps, and demonstrable public support for the conflict, not only at home but from an international coalition.[162] Another attempt to learn lessons from the history of limited warfare, to become more proficient in these conflicts rather than to avoid them, emerged in 1990, when the Marines reissued its Small Wars Manual, last published in 1940 after a series of Caribbean "banana wars."

During the Persian Gulf War (1990–1991), the desire to avoid the asymmetric conditions of Vietnam, to fight a war without the impingement of civilians, drove U.S. General Norman Schwarzkopf to outflank Iraqi forces in Kuwait and force the surrenders of surrounded units, without the need to occupy cities. Schwarzkopf's use of the *Kesselschlacht* ("cauldron battle," or encirclement) concept during Operation Desert Storm, as well as President George H.W. Bush's decision not to replace Saddam Hussein's regime, suggested that the specter of Vietnam continued to haunt the policymakers of the United States.[163] Leadership shelved the more total project of regime change in favor of a limited war to restore the status quo antebellum of Kuwaiti sovereignty.

In spite of its limited goals, the abrupt end of this Iraq war suggested to many observers a new Revolution in Military Affairs (RMA). Like the previous European revolution of the early modern period, this one was based on technological advances in weaponry. But quite unlike the fortifications and artillery of the European kingdoms, the new weapons were revolutionary in their means of communication: computer networks and satellites that coordinated weapons such as stealth jets and guided munitions. These innovations demonstrated through "shock and awe" the obsolescence of the Iraqi defenses. For the remainder of the 1990s, the United States and the U.K. imposed sanctions and deployed air forces to put pressure on the Iraqi Ba'ath regime to abide by United Nations policies.[164]

---

[162] Andrew Bacevich, *The New American Militarism: How Americans are Seduced by War* (Oxford University Press, 2013).

[163] Lawrence Freedman and Efraim Karsh, "How Kuwait Was Won: Strategy in the Gulf War," *International Security*, vol. 6, no. 2 (Fall, 1991), 5–41; Robert Scales, *Certain Victory: The U.S. Army in the Gulf War* (Potomac Books, 1998).

[164] Keith Shimko, *The Iraq Wars and America's Military Revolution* (Cambridge University Press, 2010); Thierry Gongora and Harald von Riekhoff, eds. *Toward a Revolution in Military Affairs?: Defense and Security at the Dawn of the Twenty-First Century* (Greenwood Press, 2000).

The Americans, without a near-peer threat following the collapse of the Soviet Union, nevertheless maintained a sprawling conventional force at overseas posts. The defense budget plateaued through the 1990s at around $300 billion per year, a falling percentage of GDP as the U.S. internet-based economy boomed. The 1990s saw a reduction in conventional ground forces for the United States, but the production of new aircraft and aircraft carriers, along with the cultivation of a clandestine CIA-Special Operations-contractor elite, which deployed on a constant basis to peacekeeping missions such as in Somalia and the Balkans. Since the beginning of the Global War on Terrorism, military spending climbed steadily, regardless of administration, to over $800 billion per year, or more than all countries outside of its NATO alliance combined.[165]

## 6.2 Global War on Terrorism (2001–2021)

In the early 1990s, the Saudi financier of Afghan anti-Soviet resistance Osama bin Laden founded a new organization in response to the First Intifada and the Persian Gulf War. The international group, known as Al Qaeda (the base), developed scalable political objectives. At times, bin Laden claimed only defensive measures against the occupation of holy sites in Israel and Saudi Arabia by "Jews and Crusaders," whereas his most expansive goals implied the establishment of a global caliphate modeled on the Taliban regime.[166]

Al Qaeda's attacks on the United States brought renewed global interest to asymmetric warfare. Terrorists had employed the tactic of hijacking airplanes since the 1970s, but the planes' use as missiles against symbolic targets emerged as a stunning novelty. There were, however, antecedents in Al Qaeda's campaign: the group had targeted the World Trade Center in a 1998 truck bombing, and they launched a waterborne attack on the USS *Cole* in October 2000. The disparity in resources used was the most obvious feature of the approach. On September 11, 2001, nineteen men armed with box cutters achieved their ends against an American defense industry invested with trillions of dollars in resources. The U.S. government reaction to the attacks was less a break with previous policy than an intensification of existing trends: a global deployment of forces, funded by the national debt, with basic tasks outsourced to contractors and allies. NATO, for the first time in its history, invoked the Article 5 agreement of collective defense and joined the United States in Afghanistan. As time wore on, the caveats that NATO

---

[165] Heidi Peltier, "We Get What We Pay For: The Cycle of Military Spending, Industry Power, and Economic Dependence," *Costs of War*, Brown University, June 8, 2023; SIPRI Military Expenditure Database, www.sipri.org/databases/milex.

[166] Osama bin Laden, "Declaration of Jihad Against Americans," *Al Islah*, September 2, 1996; bin Laden, "Text of Fatwa Urging Jihad Against Americans," *Al Quds Al Arabi*, February 23, 1998.

allies imposed on their forces often relegated them to governance support, policing, or training roles, rather than the offensive operations led by the United States.[167]

George W. Bush, during his presidential campaign in 2000, claimed the military should not be involved in "nation building," but should focus instead on the conventional aspects of "winning wars." In keeping with this sentiment, the Global War on Terrorism focused at first on the manhunt for bin Laden and the dismantling of his network of associates. But after his escape into Pakistan and a Taliban insurgency emerged throughout the greater Afghan borderlands, some military leaders began to propose a broader counterinsurgency (COIN) strategy. This approach included military-enabled governance, economic development, and the training of local-national security forces, as opposed to the narrower counter-terrorism means of pinpoint special operations and targeted missile attacks.

The trend toward COIN accelerated with the publication of General David Petraeus's FM 3-24, *Counterinsurgency* (2007). The manual developed theories proposed during earlier wars of decolonization by David Galula, as it empha-sized the societal problems that spawned terrorist networks. More attention shifted to intelligence gathering through the alignment of interests with locals, rather than the conventional focus on offensive, "kinetic" operations. The policy shift resulted in bitter conflicts within the U.S. establishment. Critics feared that the military had abandoned its professional competence in managing violence in favor of a "social scientist way of war." The COINdinistas, led by Petraeus, countered that conventional solutions that appeared to work well in the Second World War era were no longer relevant to the conditions where U.S. forces deployed. As soldier-historian John Nagl put it, the key task of the United States was "empowering the intimidated majority" of the populace which could provide reliable intelligence against an enemy that operated more like a "mafia crime ring" than an opposing army. Another COIN proponent, Australian Lieutenant Colonel David Kilcullen, elaborated that the Global War on Terrorism featured a hybrid nature of combatants: a hard core of "postmod-ern nihilist" international agents recruited "accidental" guerrillas in each local theater. Most fighters on the ground were "premodern traditionalists," ambiva-lent about the political goals of Al Qaeda, but who opposed military occupiers because they intruded on local ways of life.[168]

---

[167] Beth Bailey and Richard Immerman, *Understanding the U.S. Wars in Iraq and Afghanistan* (New York University Press, 2015); David P. Auerswald and Stephen M. Saideman, eds., *NATO in Afghanistan: Fighting Together, Fighting Alone* (Princeton University Press, 2014).

[168] John Nagl, *Learning to Eat Soup with a Knife: Counterinsurgency Lessons from Malaya and Vietnam* (University of Chicago Press, 2005), xiii–xiv; David Kilcullen, *The Accidental Guerrilla: Fighting Small Wars in the Midst of a Big One* (Oxford University Press, 2009), xiv–xv; for a critique of "good governance" COIN, see Jacqueline Hazelton, *Bullets Not Ballots*, 2–6.

**Figure 10** IED attack against a Stryker vehicle in Iraq, 2007, Wikimedia Commons

Technology played an inconsistent role in the Global War on Terrorism. Insurgents in some cases benefited from U.S. drone attacks, which laid bare the differences in resources between the combatant sides. Drone attacks increased throughout President Obama's years as commander-in-chief of the Global War on Terrorism (2008–2016), in the search for an asymmetric loophole in gathering intelligence and delivering lethal fires without the need to expose American soldiers to danger. Insurgents scored propaganda coups for every drone that fired on innocuous family gatherings, but even precise and "successful" drone attacks were so foreign and terrifying to local populations as to drive public sentiment away from counterinsurgent forces.[169] The insurgents' own technological advances appeared with the proliferation of improvised explosive devices (IED), as seen in Figure 10, which produced more casualties among NATO forces than any other weapon, but which also typically killed and maimed more civilians than military targets. The IED took many forms, from remote-detonated or pressure plate mines, to suicide vest (SVIED), and vehicle borne (VBIED) varieties.[170]

---

[169] For critiques from opposite sides of the political spectrum, see Lloyd Gardner, *Killing Machine: The American Presidency in the Age of Drone Warfare* (New Press, 2013), and Mark Moyar, *Strategic Failure: How President Obama's Drone Warfare, Defense Cuts, and Military Amateurism Have Imperiled America* (Simon and Schuster, 2015). See also David Edwards, *Caravan of Martyrs* (University of California Press, 2017), 148–151.

[170] Andrew Smith, *Improvised Explosive Devices in Iraq, 2003-2009: A Case of Operational Surprise and Institutional Response* (Strategic Studies Institute, 2011); James Revill, *Improvised Explosive Devices: The Paradigmatic Weapon of New Wars* (Palgrave Macmillan, 2016).

Insurgents responded to the influx of conventional units with attacks on soft targets, to include the coordination of strikes when inexperienced units arrived in theater. The rotation problem became acute in Afghanistan from 2003 to 2007. NATO allies on six- or nine-month rotations backfilled for American units redirected to the surge in Iraq, where they were sometimes "stop lossed," their tours extended from twelve to fifteen months. The Global War on Terrorism resulted in about seven thousand U.S. military deaths (and slightly more contractor deaths) in the two combat zones combined. But these numbers paled in comparison to indigenous allied military deaths – about 70,000 in Afghanistan and 50,000 in Iraq – and civilian casualties, estimated at 40,000 in Afghanistan and up to 200,000 in Iraq.[171]

The major theaters of the Global War on Terrorism shared some similarities. In both cases, hostile indigenous governments fell within weeks, following the Afghan Northern Alliance encirclement of Kabul in late 2001 and a U.S. armored "thunder run" to Baghdad in April 2003. Thereafter, insurgents claiming a religious mandate sought to demoralize the invaders and turn local people against the host-nation government through episodes of spectacular violence. But conditions of the insurgency differed in each place. In Iraq, urban centers such as Ramadi and Fallujah devolved into hotbeds of rebellion where street fighting ensued. Afghan cities, by contrast, fell within the security bubbles of the foreign coalition's Forward Operating Bases (FOBs), which left insurgents to recruit among the more numerous rural peasantry. Partisanship became a problem in both countries, though in different ways. The split was religious in Iraq, between Shi'a and Sunni militants. In Afghanistan, society fractured on ethnic lines, as dominant Pashtun families jockeyed for position among themselves within the Taliban, and with minority Tajik, Uzbek, and Hazara leaders in the Kabul-based republican government.

U.S. officials attempted to build democratic regimes in Afghanistan and in Iraq at the same time they waged war on a militant minority. Emphasis often tended toward the latter task, no matter how much leadership invoked "hearts and minds." Petraeus himself, when in mid-2010 he replaced General Stanley McChrystal as the top officer in Afghanistan, shifted policy to approve more lethal strikes on suspected insurgent locations.[172] Throughout the generation-long war in Afghanistan, the United States spent $145 billion on Afghan

---

[171] "Human Costs of post 9/11 Wars," Brown University, https://watson.brown.edu/costsofwar/figures/2021/WarDeathToll.

[172] Mark Perry, *The Pentagon's Wars: The Military's Undeclared War Against America's Presidents* (Hachette, 2017), Chapter 9; see also David Loyn, *The Long War: The Inside Story of America and Afghanistan Since 9/11* (St. Martin's, 2021).

reconstruction (of which $83 billion funded indigenous security forces). On the other hand, the U.S. government spent $837 billion on Department of Defense activities in the country, so it became evident to local leaders which entity dominated the power of the purse.[173] The excess of military money resulted in reckless spending on projects that often served to enrich elites and alienate ordinary locals.

Whereas the United States supplied almost all of the funding for the conflicts, Afghan and Iraqi fighters made up most of the manpower. Military partnership proceeded alongside programs of politics, economics, and justice. But funding disparities meant that raising indigenous military forces took priority. An array of institutions emerged to address the partnership issue. General Karl Eikenberry became a leading proponent of employing regular soldiers, rather than Special Forces, in the training effort. The U.S. 10th Mountain Brigade's Task Force Phoenix deployed in an explicit training role in the fall of 2002, as it became clear there were not enough Special Forces available to train the Afghan National Army. The United States later developed Embedded Training Teams, called Military Transition Teams (MiTT) in Iraq, to deploy alongside local national battalions. NATO allies got involved in partnership, as they created their own Operational Mentoring and Liaison Teams (OMLT). By 2004, the United States shifted institutional responsibility for Afghan training to the National Guard, which took on an increasing role in Task Force Phoenix and the Security Forces Assistance Teams (SFAT) that followed in its place. Some Special Forces units did remain in their traditional role, through a series of "local police" efforts, to include the Village Stability Operations Program, developed by Lieutenant Colonel Scott Mann.[174] This embedding of small, elite units into the countryside, similar to the Marine Corps' Vietnam-era Combined Action Platoons and European colonial practices before them, was not employed in large enough numbers to assess effectiveness. Anecdotal evidence suggested that the decentralized approach could have been a viable means of counterinsurgency. But instead of the grassroots approach, coalition resources focused on the top-down creation of large army corps and national police organizations.[175]

The United States and its NATO allies deployed a "whole of government" approach to establishing political partnerships in both Afghanistan and Iraq.

---

[173]  SIGAR, "What we need to learn: Lessons from 20 years of Afghanistan Reconstruction," August 16, 2021, 4.

[174]  Scott Mann, "Bypassing the Graveyard: a New Approach to Stabilizing Afghanistan," *Small Wars Journal*, July 30, 2014.

[175]  Mark Moyar, *Village Stability Operations and the Afghan Local Police* (Joint Special Operations University, 2014).

The Departments of State and Justice, along with aid and development organizations, deployed to mentor indigenous counterparts. Neoconservative pundit Thomas Barnett elaborated on the concept of regime change in the early post-9/11 years, whereby the goal of warfare would be to replace rogue states with new governments that agreed to become part of the "functioning core" of productive states.[176] Debates emerged from the outset about how much of a "big tent" approach the Americans should allow in these new client states: cooperation with former Ba'ath Party members in Iraq and former Taliban affiliates in Afghanistan became thorny issues. To give entrenched authorities more military resources threatened to enable them to better extract resources from their own communities, but coalition forces often saw few other choices willing and capable to govern. Over time, the United States proved willing to work with "warlord" partners who could establish security, such as General Muhammed Latif in Fallujah, and Uzbek strongman Abdul Rashid Dostum, the Vice President of Afghanistan by 2014 amid the U.S. drawdown of forces.[177] Local nationals' preferences for rapid justice and stability, whether delivered by the Taliban, a Shi'a commander, or a tribal strongman, belied Western assumptions that most people around the world would opt for "Jeffersonian democracy" if given the chance. Just as the popular account of Afghan school building *Three Cups of Tea* turned out to be fraudulent, much of the American aid flowed into the venal schemes of anti-democratic politicians, if not to criminals or insurgent forces. The growing attention to the corruption problem in Afghanistan, as President Obama's administration inherited the war in 2009, strained the Kabul government's claims to sovereignty.[178]

Of course, Americans brought about their own public relations crises, as scandals at Abu Ghraib prison in Iraq (2003), Guantanamo Bay, Cuba (2005), and Bagram, Afghanistan (2012), shook public confidence in the war effort. The post–Global War on Terrorism emergence of the Islamic State (ISIS) in Iraq, together with the Taliban takeover of Afghanistan in September 2021, points to the insufficiency of the military attempts to provoke fundamental societal change. Presumptive solutions imposed from above and abroad seem only to

---

[176] Thomas Barnett, *The Pentagon's New Map: War and Peace in the Twenty-First Century* (Penguin, 2004).

[177] Thomas Barfield, *Afghanistan: A Cultural and Political History* (Princeton University Press, 2010), 218–220, 250–251; Ali Allawi, *The Occupation of Iraq: Winning the War, Losing the Peace* (Yale University Press, 2008), 278.

[178] Jon Krakauer, *Three Cups of Deceit: How Greg Mortenson, Humanitarian Hero, Lost His Way* (Byliner, 2011); Craig Whitlock, *The Afghanistan Papers: A Secret History of the War* (Simon and Schuster, 2021); Carter Malkasian, *The American War in Afghanistan: A History* (Oxford University Press, 2021), 231–233.

have inflamed perceptions of neo-imperial meddling and apostasy across wide swaths of the world.

## 7 Leveling the Asymmetric Battlefield: Technology, Intelligence, and Law

Since the middle of the 20th century, insurgent forces have experienced greater success against stronger military occupiers, a trend that throws into question the value of conventional state power. The weaker combatant forces have leveled the playing field through the neutralization of the military technology gap, adoption of new media strategies, and changing legal norms that restricted uses of state violence and granted legitimacy to non-state resistance movements.

The weapons technology gap has been the most apparent distinction between conventional and asymmetric wars. In cases where one combatant side has produced a set of weapons for which there is no defense – especially naval, aerial, or nuclear weapons – the opposing side has sought other means of resistance, whether through unconventional military attacks or from a popular political cause. Scientific innovation throughout the modern era has tended to lend state forces an advantage over insurgent peoples, though the latter have selectively integrated foreign technologies into existing martial frameworks: from Native Americans' use of repeating rifles in the 19th century, to the proliferation of the Soviet AK-47 assault rifle in the 20th century, to *jihadi* uses of improvised explosive devices in the 21st. The IED in particular showed how a piece of "low" tech, a makeshift bomb detonated by a cheap cell phone or a pressure plate, could disrupt the more elaborate technologies of U.S. armored vehicles.

Advances in media technology, on the other hand, have tended to favor insurgencies over their opponents. The means of spreading awareness about resistance against a stronger military opponent has become easier in recent decades, though informative media have long been weaponized. Early in the modern era, journals and pamphlets used the nation as an organizing concept of rebellion to a growing literate class. During the Age of Revolutions, Thomas Paine captured an inchoate sense of dissent against the British Empire with his popular "Common Sense." Insurgent leader Francisco de Miranda likewise carried a printing press into Venezuela as a means of resistance against the Spanish Empire.[179] Paine and Miranda framed their discourses in terms of national liberation, which became an even more significant concept as innovations in radio and film spread political consciousness to less literate

---

[179] Sophia Rosenfeld, *Common Sense: A Political History* (Harvard University Press, 2011); Adelman, "Age of Imperial Revolutions," 319.

populations. Though 20th-century communist revolutionaries used class-based internationalist rhetoric, the history of Southeast Asia suggests that national sentiment continued to trump economics as a motivation for war. Hence, a newly unified Vietnam soon found itself fighting wars against neighboring communist regimes in Cambodia and China. Media consumers throughout the modern era have sorted themselves into imagined communities, whose exploits animated ongoing epics, in competition against other nations, projected toward glorious futures.[180]

The digital age has brought renewed attention to medium and message as they pertain to warfare. Previous forms of mass communication required the resources to run a printing press, build radio transmitters, or produce a film. The internet's relative lack of material requirements for publication compared to earlier media technologies has enabled mass reporting from conflict zones and instantaneous, global sharing of content. Whereas political theorist Hannah Arendt noted that totalitarian governments of the 20th century immobilized subject populations through censorship, the past two decades have revealed that an abundance of information can paralyze political thought and action just as well.[181] Yet the internet has both democratized and splintered the ability of insurgent groups to spread propaganda. Through social media, it has never been easier for insurgents to broadcast their causes across enormous platforms. But it has also never been easier to dismiss any given fact as "fake news," or to propose alternate narratives. Nor before have a few gatekeepers at social media platforms, a much smaller group than the corps of publishers of the previous century, been equipped with algorithms to hide speech deemed dangerous and to champion their few, curated causes.

The digital realm has proven a difficult space for coalition building. Although internet users enjoy seamless connection via data, they tend to be physically isolated and to react in superficial ways.[182] For all the assumed advantages of the worldwide web for military underdogs, state agents can use social media to their own advantages, either by buying influence with key spokespeople, or by infiltrating the information space with competing messages, usually along Thermidorian lines of restoring order. State forces capable of shutting down electricity or internet

---

[180] Benedict Anderson, *Imagined Communities: Reflections on the Origin and Spread of Nationalism* (Verso, 1983), 1–4; Marshall McLuhan, *Understanding Media: The Extensions of Man* (MIT Press, 1964), Chapter 1.

[181] See discussion of Arendt's comment in David Ucko, *The Insurgent's Dilemma: A Struggle to Prevail* (Oxford: Oxford University Press, 2022), Chapter 7.

[182] Jan van Dijk and Kenneth Hacker, *Internet and Democracy in the Network Society* (Routledge, 2018).

connectivity in a region for more than a few days threaten to return the spread of information to the energy levels of charismatic coalition-builders.

Nevertheless, it is unlikely that any state power can succeed in controlling many of the decentralized nodes of the internet for long. The faster information spreads from a conflict zone, the more difficult it may be for the stronger foreign military power to maintain operations abroad. And the battle for cyberspace appears to grow more significant as time goes on. Recent developments in computer science have shifted the basis of economic value from material to information. If the age of political revolutions that began in the late 18th century ditched divine rights in favor of human rights as the ultimate ends of war, the internet revolution of the late 20th century has perhaps already replaced human values with data control as the primary pursuit of conflict.[183]

Theorists have long emphasized intelligence-gathering as the primary function of asymmetric warfare, in which the counterinsurgent struggles more to find the enemy than to fight him. The imperative to glean intelligence, however, does not always imply beneficent treatment of an entire society, which everywhere breaks up into self-interested segments. The counterinsurgent may woo just a few local elites in order to gain access to informants and pools of indigenous manpower. The majority of the populations caught up in asymmetric wars have therefore been less likely to benefit from aid development as to suffer the results of harsh measures of state control and victimization at the hands of anti-government terrorists. Advancements in satellites, drones, and other surveillance technology appear to have granted counterinsurgents more effective tools of submission. However, this augmented data production may be useless, or indeed harmful to understanding, if absent the appropriate framing and interpretation by indigenous informants.

States have tried to define warfare in advantageous legal terms since the days of jurist Francis Lieber in the mid 19th century. His American Civil War code adopted a humanitarian tone in order to justify the underlying legal principle: that only established political states had recourse to violence, and that all attempts by citizens to wage their own private wars by sabotage or "bushwhacking" were to be punished by summary execution. The experience of the Allies during the Second World War, however, made signatories to the subsequent Geneva Conventions (1949) sensitive to the rights of resistance movement members. The postwar state system led by United States, Britain, and France, to the exclusion of their wartime allies in China and the U.S.S.R., coalesced around a commitment to support "free" peoples who rebelled against fascist or

---

[183] Yuval Harari has done some informed speculation about post-humanist ideologies in *Homo Deus: A Brief History of Tomorrow* (Harvill Secker, 2015).

communist dictatorships, and at the same time sought to limit the ability of states to oppose rebellion by collective punishment, forced migration, mass imprisonment, and execution, all of which had been in common practice up to that point.

Imperial agents throughout the modern era have emphasized their adherence to international law as justification for persistence against popular rebellions. During the Age of Revolutions, British officials referred to their "empire of humanity," much like French revolutionaries who framed their monarchist foes as enemies of liberty, and therefore of all mankind. More recently, support for the United States after the September 11, 2001, attacks, and interstate solidarity for Israel for its operations against Hamas and other militant organizations after October 7, 2023, suggest that state agents will continue to use the inhumane tactics of their opponents as a way to rally support for prolonged military operations. On the other hand, forces that find themselves opposed to hegemonic military powers today have begun to use "lawfare" to their own ends. Palestinians' calls for war crimes trials against Israelis and divestment from their economic enterprises, as well as China's legal attempts to block access to its coastal seas, represent a potential turning of the litigious tide against stronger states.[184]

While governments claim to abide by international humanitarian agreements, commanders on the ground often disregard legalities in the service of military necessity. At the tactical level, some military practitioners question the development of norms against assassination, hostage-taking, torture, and the use of chemical or nuclear weapons. They insist that tactics must match the enemy in question, and they rail against politicians who dare to limit their militaries in times of war.[185] Yet the heavy-handedness of counterinsurgents has tended to play into the hands of the weaker military side, in terms of information operations (IO) victories.

Asymmetric wars have been a mainstay of modernity, defined as separation from the ancient era and from the state of nature. Scientific attempts to manage the environment and to progress beyond the ancients have driven the massive disparities in military technology evident today. Moreover, the assumption of modernity by combatants on one side of a conflict has become a justification to wage "savage wars of peace," to use Rudyard Kipling's idiom.[186] Since Kipling's era, strong military powers have shifted rhetoric away from beneficent

---

[184] Orde Kittrie, *Lawfare: Law as a Weapon of War* (Oxford University Press, 2016).

[185] Roger Trinquier, *Modern Warfare: A French View of Counterinsurgency* (DIANE, 1964), 20–22.

[186] Max Boot, *The Savage Wars of Peace: Small Wars and the Rise of American Power* (Basic Books, 2014).

empire, toward guarantees of free trade and human rights. But the fundamental asymmetries of resources and firepower have only increased. In military terms, the rich have gotten richer. The resources of today's states have taken on an absurd array of weaponry, delivered in ever more abstracted ways from the counterinsurgent's society, now insulated from the effects of war by the constant deployment of a professional military-technical class.[187]

At present, the NATO powers prepare for war against revisionist states in China, Russia, and Iran, each of which has its own set of historical grievances against one or more of the North Atlantic states. The Chinese advocacy of "Unrestricted Warfare," Russian uses of paramilitary units and social media manipulation, and Iranian sponsorship of terrorist proxies throughout the Middle East are responses to grievances against opponents that have been irresistible in military terms. The problems that unconventional tactics and anti-foreigner propaganda can cause strong military forces have become evident in recent decades. On the other hand, state forces armed with a narrative of eliminating extremists – along with the capacity to control electricity, food, or water in a given area – allow for occupiers to claim after operations, no matter how much destruction preceded, to have redeemed a war-torn region back into the camp of the moderns. These fundamental motivations for weak and strong powers to participate in asymmetric warfare have brought about a series of conflicts, whose ubiquity suggests they are an inherent element of the modern state system. The widening disparity of resources between the United States and its discontents suggests that warfare of the future will continue to be asymmetric in nature.[188]

---

[187] Andrew Bacevich, ed., *The Long War: A New History of U.S. National Security Policy Since World War II* (Columbia University Press, 2007).

[188] Ilan Berman, ed., *The Logic of Irregular War: Asymmetry and America's Adversaries* (Rowman and Littlefield, 2017).

For EU product safety concerns, contact us at Calle de José Abascal, 56–1°, 28003 Madrid, Spain or eugpsr@cambridge.org.

www.ingramcontent.com/pod-product-compliance
Ingram Content Group UK Ltd.
Pitfield, Milton Keynes, MK11 3LW, UK
UKHW021839150525
458487UK00018B/351